Miranda Roberts is one half of the team that set up Shrimpy, the seafood-based street-food stall. After seven years of running Shrimpy successfully, and sometimes not so successfully, she's learned a thing or two about what can make an idea work and what can make it fail. Prior to setting up Shrimpy she developed valuable skills for street food while in restaurant management. Before that, her professional love affair with food began while working on Nigella Lawson's Christmas show.

You can usually find her in the back of her van eating street food and claiming that it's the best meal she's ever had. She makes that claim a lot.

Delicious Freedom

How to take your street-food business
from dream to reality

....

Miranda Roberts

A How To book

ROBINSON

ROBINSON

First published in Great Britain in
2021 by Robinson

10 9 8 7 6 5 4 3 2 1

A CIP catalogue record for this book
is available from the British Library.

ISBN: 978-1-47214-527-7

Typeset in Sentinel and Scala Sans
by Ian Hughes

Printed and bound in Great Britain by
Clays Ltd, Elcograf S.p.A.

Papers used by Robinson are from
well-managed forests and other
responsible sources.

MIX
Paper from
responsible sources
FSC® C104740

Robinson
An imprint of
Little, Brown Book Group
Carmelite House
50 Victoria Embankment
London EC4Y 0DZ

An Hachette UK Company
www.hachette.co.uk

www.littlebrown.co.uk

How To Books are published by
Robinson, an imprint of Little,
Brown Book Group. We welcome
proposals from authors who have
first-hand experience of their
subjects. Please set out the aims
of your book, its target market and
its suggested contents in an email
to howto@littlebrown.co.uk.

To Stefan,
thanks for riding the bus with me.

Contents

Introduction

On the street with Shrimpy

Street food is the most accessible way to set up your own food business, be your own boss and make your own money. You don't need £50,000 to sink into setting up a restaurant which, let's be honest, you wouldn't know how to run, or the inclination to sign ten years of your life away on an idea that you've been thinking about in the bath.

All you need is a decent recipe and willingness to put the hours in; the rest you can learn on the job. The sheer amount of stuff you'll learn after a few months is ridiculous. You'll feel like a superhero (you're not a superhero).

I've learnt more in the last ten years than I had done in my whole previous lifetime. That's the best part: you learn everything, from how to change a tyre on a Transit in the middle of the night, how corporation tax works, cooking equipment, and how to deal with someone's emotional issue at work, to team building, and to presentation being everything. You learn how to deal with personal issues because there are so many problems at work that you know how to deal with them. I used to be panicked and now I'm very chilled, and I know that there's always a way through and when anything shit happens something good always comes out of it.'

Anna and Tony, ANNA MAE'S

_____

Don't let the repetition of problems put you off. You are, after all:

a) Setting this up from scratch, and

b) Probably going to encounter all sorts of people and have to deal with uncomfortable situations.

Both these things will present their own problems: people can be a bit shit and you will be a bit shit at the start, so the earlier you understand that, the easier it will be to get on and do a better job.

Street food enables people to show off skills that just ten years ago they might not have been able to because it's pretty simple and relatively cheap to just give it a go. And that's it: just give it a go. You don't have to throw your whole life away; you can do it alongside your real job and see how it feels. Will it be hard work? Of course, but it'll be *so exciting*! Stop wasting away your weekends being hungover and watching Netflix. Get out there and give it a go! Who knows what may happen!

What do we do? How do we do it?

I spend a lot of my life on markets and at events with my partner and our staff. People often ask us for advice.

'I'm sick of the rat race.' 'I've got an idea that will actually change people's lives.' 'I really love crumpets/kimchi/hot dogs! I want to share this love with the world. How do I do it? Where do I start?' We've heard it all.

The people who ask this are on the right track, going to an actual market and looking around, seeing the footfall and talking to traders. Some of them will have inferred from Instagram that this market is *the* place to be with the best people and the busiest traders, but Instagram is a picture book of lies. They see the busy market, the amazing colours, the cool festivals and the epic shots of food porn. They believe what you, the trader, want to believe: that this street gig is the centre of the universe and berate themselves, 'God, if I'm not down there every week what am I doing with myself?'

What they're not seeing is the rubbish spot you slog it out in for six months before you get a chance at the busy main street. They don't see the dodgy festival electricity that keeps tripping out and closing you down. They don't wait for the failed delivery that sends you half the portions you need to make enough money to pay your rent.

What they do see is the joy, and there's some of that too. It's great to spend time in fields dressed up to the nines drinking beers with your mates after a crazy day trading at a festival. The other part is an absolute nightmare. That's when your gazebo blows away in the same storm you set up in, everything's covered in mud, you're sitting on £1,500 worth of rotting stock and your world is falling apart around you. The field: great. The beer: great. But the storm is shit. You need to be aware of the good *and* the bad.

'When street food is working and successful it's the best job in the world; it's the greatest buzz because all my decisions have resulted in this working well. I'm outside, I'm talking to people, everyone's happy, it's wonderful. But when it doesn't work it's absolutely horrible.'

Dave, TACO DAVE

Street food can make you a living, but it's not an easy way to get rich. You might make silly money one week, but that has to keep you going while you're losing money stood in the rain the next. It's hard work, great fun, hand-to-mouth, well-paid, heart-breaking, a creative outlet, heavy manual labour, soul-destroying, life-affirming, a chance to be your own boss and a chance to develop a real obsession with the weather forecast. And all that in an average day.

But don't despair. If you want it, don't doubt yourself. You've had the idea and that's pretty much all you need. Every business you see, no matter how small or mundane, was set up by someone thinking, 'Hey, I could do that better than them', or 'Why's no one doing this? I can give the people what they want!' Set it up, give it a go and see where it takes you. If there's no one else doing it, then you're automatically the best person for the job, you're already one step ahead of the crowd. And believe me, there are people with far less intelligence or experience than you out there doing it already. Go ahead, dream big.

Why do we do it?

People sometimes say to me, 'You're doing my dream job', which can be an odd thing to hear when you've been up since 4 a.m. and have oil down your jeans. Other times friends ask me, 'Why do you bother?', after hearing me moan about every single aspect of the business over too many bottles of wine. And the reason is delicious freedom.

The freedom is amazing. You can do what the hell you like. When we chucked in our jobs to start Shrimpy I kept expecting someone to stop me and say, 'Excuse me, stop this. What are you doing? Who told you you could do this?' I'd been through school, sixth form, university, an internship and several jobs, so even the thought that I'd leave the pre-destined map of 'what you need to do next' was mad. It took me ages to shake the feeling that someone was going to tell us, 'Enough now, get back to work'. But once you're rid of that, the freedom is fantastic. Yes, you'll work longer and harder than you ever have for anyone else. Yes, you will have sleepless nights and stress about things that you never knew it was possible to stress about. But you get to choose it all. Every single event or market you can choose to do or not. You can choose what your branding is, choose who you are as a business, choose who you work with. If you don't like something, you can just get rid of it or not do it again. It's like paying off a mortgage on a house – every piece of work you do improves your business. And it could also literally pay off your mortgage. Everything is working towards 'the bigger picture', whatever that may be for you.

You will be surrounded by top-notch, delicious food all the time, which is a huge perk. Those soggy lunchtime sandwiches are a thing of the past; you'll be able to eat around the world every damn day. You end up taking this for granted and assume that everyone eats this well all the time. It can completely ruin going out for a nice meal with your mates as you probably had something better for your lunch, sitting in the back of your van. You are surrounded by people who are at the top of their game, most of whom are just focusing on one recipe, so you know it's really good. The best pad thai I've ever eaten was made in a gazebo and I've eaten things while knee-deep in mud at festivals that have blown my mind. Some of the best places to eat across the country are in glorified market halls, which would have been a completely mad thing to say ten years ago. Street food has enabled people to give it a go, people who, perhaps due to lack of money or experience, wouldn't have had the chance to get into food any other way. And in doing so they have spruced up our car parks, market halls and manky street corners. They have improved our communities.

The financial crash in 2007–2008 led to the birth of British street food. People were looking for ways to be independent, make their own money and get started with relatively low capital. Who knows what the world will look like after Covid-19, but it's not that much of a stretch to imagine that there will be another resurgence. Street-food businesses are well placed to survive tough times compared to restaurants. If a street-food business has to close for a period, it has fewer regular overheads than a restaurant and so there is less money going out of the account. If we *can* weather the storm, then once it's all over we can just set up our gazebos and start again.

Not all restaurants succeed, leaving a lot of skilled chefs, waiters and managers looking for work. Having been burnt too many times working for others, they might be considering going out on their own, to take charge of their own destiny. You might be one of them, or perhaps you have spent countless hours testing and improving your signature dish to such a point that you think that it's worth a shot. Being stuck indoors, as we were during lockdown in 2020, will have made it clear to a lot of people what they think is important in life and what they truly enjoy doing. Maybe you've had a sudden realisation about just how precious life is and you've come out of your front door screaming, 'You only live once, guys – live your dreams!' Whatever the reason you've decided to pick up this book, you are welcome here.

One and a half billion people across the world eat street food every day. It encompasses many things, and can be done just about anywhere. The great thing about selling food is that people need to eat. It is a necessity. There are lots of hurdles to tackle with food businesses, and they can be difficult to run, but always remember that people do need to eat. They don't need to buy a candle every day, they don't need a manicure every day, but they do need to eat three meals a day, so why not have one of them be with you?

There are big, exciting opportunities out there for people who have the drive and determination to make it work. You don't need much experience; as long as you're relatively sensible, then you can make it work. The beauty of street food is that, if you're clever, you can couple the decent profit margins with the low overheads and make a decent life for yourself.

And, of course, why the hell not? Life is exciting, don't spend all of it on a shitty commute to a strip-lit office. If there's something you're passionate about, go and do it. It gets harder as you get older, as you tend to have more responsibilities, but there are always possibilities out there. You don't have to go hard or go home; you can give things a go carefully. Don't be miserable and just think *What if?*; go and do it. In the end, as long as you're relatively sensible, then the worst that can happen is that it goes tits up and you have to go back to your old job. The beauty of street food is that if a location doesn't work, then you just pack up and try somewhere else. You're not tied to a five- or ten-year lease. Life is strange: priorities can dramatically change within just a few years, in which case you can pack up and go, but you'll have given it a good shot.

'I haven't worked for anyone now for eight years. I've been to loads of amazing places, met loads of amazing people, had loads of amazing experiences and it's all been off my own bat. I've been able to decide what I want to do.'

Beth and Jim, SEADOG

Read this

This guide gives you an insight into the world of street food so that you've got a better chance of making the right choice when you chuck in your secure job. I'm offering you advice and stories from my experience as a trader and from other traders. I'm not perfect and I'm certainly not a millionaire, but I've got some hindsight and loads of experience. You can always go it alone and live and learn, but I'd like to try to help you not to lose £10,000 while you're learning.

Read the advice. It might not make your life easier, but it should save you time and money.

How we're going to make your idea better

I was told many stories while researching this book about how crap everyone's first set-up was. These are all great stories and give everything a lovely rose-tinted view of the past, but they're not particularly helpful now. Due to the massive boom in street food in the last ten years there are now fewer places you can actually mess up at and start from scratch. We started with a £15-a-day food stall, a tiny teppanyaki plate, a few bowls and a chalkboard, and, honestly, that wouldn't get us anywhere now.

Lots of sites are competitively priced with long waiting lists. However, there's no need to panic and start selling the family jewels; you don't need to spend thousands of pounds, but you do need to have thought about certain aspects of the business before you start, and this is where this book comes in. I'll guide you through the different aspects of the street-food game so that when you do get a chance at a pitch you are in the best possible shape to make a good impression.

One of the many great things about street food is that it has a low-cost entry point, but it's also that very thing which can bring the quality down: everyone can give it a go, but statistically not everyone will be good at it. Not everyone will be using the best ingredients, will have thought about branding, will really care that much about health and safety or be organised enough to make it the best it's going to be. This book's aim is not to make everyone the same, but to help elevate your idea, to get you to think about every part of your business and make it, hopefully, more of a success.

People tend to avoid business plans because they sound like homework. They're requested by banks and landlords for a reason: it shows that you've thought about every aspect of the business and figured out how to make it work. This book is just that. I'm going to go through all the key factors in a business plan, so that when you come to doing your own it feels easy because you'll have already thought about it.

After reading this book you should write out a basic plan. We spent a year floundering because we had NO IDEA what we were doing. We just thought it would all be an instant success (for some mad reason) and that it'd be fine, but (surprisingly) trying to sell fish sandwiches in Camden Market wasn't quite as much of a hit as we'd hoped. If we had written a business plan, it would have made us think about our customer base so much earlier than we did. Just start with the bits you know and go from there. Do it backwards for all I care, just don't feel overwhelmed by it. Stop banging on about it to your nice friends; they really don't care. See the business plan as a friend who you can discuss every aspect of the business with. Don't worry that you're not sure about some aspects or that others are wrong. What you write isn't set in stone. You can change it all down the line – think of it as market research. You're thinking about this business anyway, so you might as well think about it in a productive way – and you've bought this book, so you're clearly keen for it to be a success.

'Do a business plan, write it down. If it doesn't make sense on paper, then it's not going to work out in reality. Writing it all down gives you the answers to the things you've been worrying about in your head. It's like putting together a puzzle – you don't have to have all the answers at the start and you can start in the middle if you like, but once you start it, you'll figure out the answers along the way. And if it doesn't make financial sense on paper, then it's not going to work in real life.'

Carol, DEENEY'S

You need to be aware of every aspect of your business in order to make it work. That's why it's so annoying when you see chefs swaggering around markets telling people how authentic their food is but it's just that people don't 'understand' it so they have to 'dumb it down'. Dear Lord, give me strength. Don't patronise your customers. It's true that some will get it and others won't, but give yourself the best possible shot by doing your research and making it accessible. Think about the location you are in and whether the food suits the location. It's not rocket science. Leave your ego at the door, do a business plan and visit some street-food events. See what works and find out why.

Just because the scene is better than it was ten years ago, don't worry about being perfect from the get-go. If we all waited until we were perfect to do anything, then we'd still be sitting at home. Don't be put off by the seemingly brilliant people out there. Some of them are of course great, but don't think it was all plain sailing for them. If they say they've never done a duff event, they're just lying. Supposedly perfect people are annoying to be around, there's no fun in brilliance. The most interesting people are those who have done stuff, got it wrong and given it another go. No great anecdote has ever come out of someone being an instant success. You need to relish the process rather than the rewards. If you don't enjoy cooking or chatting to people, then this probably isn't the game for you.

Disclaimer: I didn't go to business school. I didn't even do business GCSE. This is all stuff I've learnt along the way. If you're looking for a book about in-depth business techniques or management styles, please go elsewhere. This is for those of you who know barely anything about business and are in this for the independence, creativity, fun and the street-food life. We're all making it up as we go along. I just wrote it down. Welcome aboard and enjoy it.

Chapter 1

Welcome to street food

Anyone can do it

Street food can encompass so many things. Depending on who you speak to, street food can be painfully cool venues with beers and neon lights, or it can be wholesome, salt-of-the-earth products on a farmers' market, or someone selling bacon butties outside your office. It is essentially just selling food on the street but it's the who, what, how, where and why that make it interesting and varied. There's a spot for anyone.

Who?

- Who are you? You could be anyone; you don't have to have fifty grand to spend on a vintage van (and it's probably better if you don't do that straight away anyway).

- Who are you going to work with? What does this mean for your brand? Are you using only locally sourced ingredients or are you bringing something you can't get where you are? Who your suppliers are says a lot about your business.

What?

- What are you selling?

- What are you passionate about? Is there something you want to teach people?

- What's missing from your neighbourhood?

- What is your USP? Start-up costs are minimal, so there's plenty of competition out there. You need to stand out from the crowd and be the very best you can be.

- What are your skills? How do they elevate your business? There are a lot of hats to wear at the start and for quite a while after that too, so you need to be an all-rounder. You need to be able to cook, clean, chat and balance the books at the end of the day. Some of this will come naturally, other parts less so, but you've got to put the work in; there's no point sticking your head in the sand because these things won't go away.

How?

- How are you going to make money? Will you do all weekly markets? All the festivals? Are you going to do it full time or just Saturdays?

- How are you going to operate? Will you use a gazebo? A van? A trailer?

Where?

- There are myriad options: amazing food markets with flashy neon lights and loud music, farmers' markets across the country every Saturday morning; there's Glastonbury, the Chelsea Flower Show, weddings, train stations, churchyards, car parks, school fêtes and birthday parties in back gardens.

- Are you city-based or out in the country? If city-based you may think travelling further than ten miles is a stretch, but in the countryside you'll be willing to go across counties in search of decent spots.

Why?

- Why are you doing this? What do you want out of it? Do you want to grow into a restaurant and set up an empire? Do you want more control over your time? Do you just love the market around the corner from your house and want to be part of it?

You can make thousands of different businesses by choosing different criteria from these lists, and all are valid. It would not do for us all to be the same. There's absolutely no point in having all new street-food businesses decide they need to buy the same van, get a neon sign and some branded caps and rock up at the same market. It'd be boring and actually only one of you would get a spot.

Don't be put off by the high spec of some of the events either.

Street food is about authenticity. People will buy into you as a business so much more if it's clear where their money is going. People spend their money with small businesses for many reasons, and one of them is for the story. They can see you improve week after week. They feel like they are investing in you as a person and are on the journey with you. They can actually see the £8 they give you for their sandwich being reinvested in the business; they see you get a better gazebo, another member of staff and then better branding. People love that stuff. They don't believe it when you start off with a branded truck worth £50,000. You might look cool but you lack the authenticity. People want to be part of your journey, they want to say, 'I was there at the beginning.'

A few notes to start off with

- The film *Chef* is not a documentary. Don't expect it to be as easy or as simple as Jon Favreau makes it look.

- Just because you went on holiday somewhere once does not mean you are entitled to make money by selling food from that country. Do you not think that *maybe* someone else would be better at it? Take inspiration, sure. We all have to get ideas from somewhere, but don't have the stall set up with flags and national dress and the words 'authentic' all over the menu when really you've spent more of your life in Tesco than the place you're selling 'authentic' food from.

- Don't be fooled by the long queues. Think about it sensibly: for every lovely spring day, there are three horrific winter shifts where your feet are soaked from morning through to closing, and you just manage to cover your costs if you're lucky. Don't think the path is paved with gold; there's money to be made, but it's certainly not a way to get rich quick.

First things first

Before you do anything at all, before you buy one piece of equipment or register your domain name, try to get some experience working on a street-food stall. Street-food stalls always need staff. The jobs they'll get you to do will be pretty simple, so don't panic that you won't be skilled enough. When you're trying to organise this, explain who you are and why you want to do it. If you are able to, offer yourself for free. You'll be a much more appealing prospect to a street-food trader who's knackered and trying to weigh up the costs of getting in an extra pair of inexperienced hands.

Even just one or two shifts will show you the different aspects of the business. The cooking, the manual labour, chatting to customers, dealing with the weather, being on your feet all day, learning about stock control, how to maintain hygiene levels outside, dealing with being busy, dealing with being quiet, working with other traders. The list goes on. All this stuff will be what your life revolves around if you choose to go ahead. Give it a go, see if you like it.

I once had someone come and do this. They spent the whole time talking about what kind of coat they'd need, and by the end of it had actually worked out that they didn't want to do it at all. Perfect, one shift saved them hundreds of pounds and months of work.

'I always cooked a lot at home. I loved it and did it a lot, but I had no professional experience. Just after I started Yum Bun I worked in a café one day a week as a chef because I wanted to understand how a professional kitchen works... I would definitely recommend working somewhere good for six months so that you can understand the systems and understand about where to buy things, costs, etc, because actually there's quite a lot you can shortcut with a little bit of knowledge and help to avoid costly mistakes from the start.'

Lisa, YUM BUN

And remember...
Your first few weeks of trading are going to be a shitshow. You'll make mistakes, you'll waste money and you'll suddenly see all the work you need to put in.

It's fine, it's perfectly normal, you've just got to keep plugging away. The most successful street-food traders have at least a few of the following traits:

1. Sheer bloody determination and resilience
You need to know that when you do get knocked back, or if

something goes terribly wrong, you can carry on fighting. It may rain every Saturday the whole summer; your van might break down; stock gets ruined; staff are unreliable; and, I dunno, maybe there's a global epidemic and people are banned from going outside. Who knows? The list is endless and sometimes they can all happen at once. You've got to be able to pick yourself up and keep trying.

2. Work really, really hard
It's physically tiring setting up and packing down a stall every day. You're on your feet constantly and when you get home there are often another seven jobs you need to do. At the start you've got to be every aspect of the company: chef, driver, accountant, PR manager, HR manager, operations manager – the whole shebang. And people expect you to be really good at them all, which is, of course, impossible.

3. Learn from others
You're not going to know how to do everything, so don't pretend you do. Ask for advice and take it. Employ people who are better than you and learn from them; that's the only way to truly take your business to the next level. You'll need expertise, so listen to what people say. You are not omnipotent.

4. Blind faith
All entrepreneurs need to be slightly unhinged. You have to see something others cannot. That's why you're in this position in the first place. Despite the naysayers and all the setbacks, you've still got to have faith that it'll all work out in the end.

'My main advice would be don't let people tell you that it won't work. There are so many people out there, even just friends and family, who have your best interests at heart, but they can't see what you see, so they can be overly cautious and just tell you how it can go wrong, but you need to believe in your idea."

Alex, PINK PEPPERCORN

In other words, don't let the bastards grind you down.

KEY POINTS

- Anyone can give it a go.

- It's useful to get experience.

- It's hard work.

Chapter 2

What will you sell?

Okay, so you have a family recipe you need to share with the world. Perhaps you're a chef who wants to show off your skills. Or you just think you can make a burger better than the hundreds of other burger places out there. Fine. You like it, your best friend likes it and your dog is pretty keen too. What next?

Skills

Show them off or learn some new ones – either way don't just get everything out of a pack and heat it up. A monkey could do that and you're better than that. If you're doing that, how are you different from anyone else? I knew a guy who once worked in a well-known pub-chain kitchen where even the poached eggs came in microwavable bags. If you're supporting that kind of culture, where a robot could replace you any minute, then we may as well all just lay down our tools and let the robots take over because *what's the point?*

'There are some things you can cheat and get away with, or it's just easier, but if the main part of your dish is a cheat, give up now. For example, buy mayo. You don't need to be making your own mayo and, for street

food, it can be a health and safety risk. Use sriracha because sriracha is delicious, but at least have some pride. You need to elevate everything you use.'

Dave, TACO DAVE

There's a lot of competition out there. You need to stand out and show off. People love it when you have a skill or speciality, it makes you interesting and pretty damn sexy. You need flair and swagger in street food. Use everything you've got.

Get everyone together for dinner

Present friends and family with a few different options of what your idea is and try to get honest feedback. Don't be a dick if people don't see what you see. All opinions are valid. Invite a range of people – not just your super-foodie friends, but also the ones who are happy with a plain cheese sandwich for lunch. Their opinion is equally important; you don't have to do everything they say, but listen to them. Not every person who comes to your stall is going to be a connoisseur. If you've created something that your family and friends don't understand, it's pretty much guaranteed that 75 per cent of your customers won't understand it either. Remember, you're going to be selling on the streets. Yes, it needs to be great, new and interesting, but if you want to pay your rent it also needs to be accessible. By all means, once you're a huge success and have set up a restaurant, put what you like on the menu, but bear in mind the limitations of street food. These include, but are not limited to, space, time and money. If you don't want to lower your bar, then go and be a Michelin-starred chef and you can be as flamboyant as you like, but if you're selling in a field alongside eighty other traders and you need to make back your £5,000 costs, then it needs to be at least vaguely accessible. Otherwise you've got to hope that you've already made your name as a top chef and can get into the VIP section of the foodie festivals. For the rest of you? You're screwed.

Take notes

What are people saying? How does it taste? How does it look? How are you going to serve it? How do people react to it? Is it easy to eat? Do you need a bath afterwards? Can you eat it standing up with a beer in your other hand? Do you stink after eating it? Do you have to use cutlery? Is it a meal?

Every aspect needs to be taken into account. Despite the penchant for dirty messy burgers on Instagram, people don't actually want to be covered in their food. Some will be going back to work after eating, others will be at a festival looking to pull; neither wants onions or a chipotle stain down their shirt.

'Make sure that you have your product down before you start. That is the most important thing. The brand is important, but no one is going to come back week after week for good branding; they come back for the product. You can have everything else in place, funding and the most swanky-looking van, but none of it matters; your product needs to be good and consistently good. Get your product down to a fine art and streamlined.'

Sophia, NONNA'S GELATO

Learn on the go

Whether you take everything on board or completely ignore it all, your original product will undoubtedly change. No matter how honest your friends are, nothing compares to actually trying to sell the food on the streets. Within about an hour of your first trading day you'll work out that certain aspects are or aren't working. Your product might take too long to prepare, or it might be just too complicated to do once you throw wind into the mix. People keep asking for it without the coriander. People don't buy it because it looks too messy to eat. There's too much smoke when you're cooking, so people aren't coming to your stall. People don't understand what it actually is. They don't think it's big enough, or it's just not quite right for the time of day. The list goes on.

Once you've started selling, look around. Street food is amazing because you can look directly into other people's whole operation. See how other traders operate. What makes them successful? What do their stalls look like? How are their menus worded? What's their signage like? How long is it taking them to serve people compared to you? There is so much more to a successful street-food stall than just the food. At the start you should be a sponge, soaking up ideas everywhere you see them. You can get inspiration everywhere: look in your local coffee shop – how do they run everything when they're busy? How many staff do they have? Once you start looking you'll realise that a lot of businesses have amazing solutions for day-to-day issues.

'The night before I found out that there was no electricity, so suddenly had to find a generator. It was also really hot, and I was selling a Scottish fish soup which strangely no one wanted in 30-degree heat. Thankfully there were a lot of homeless people in the graveyard so at least it wasn't wasted. It was a massive learning curve. I saw those first three weeks as market research to figure out what people want, what I need to do, and how it all works.'

Carol, DEENEY'S

The general public will give you plenty of feedback, solicited or not. They are pretty free and easy with their comments and facial expressions. The number of times people will talk about your food, your business and sometimes even you as if you aren't standing there is baffling. There will, of course, be the odd few who come and say ecstatically, 'I've been looking for something exactly like this for ages, I'm so pleased that you exist!' You will cling to these people like life rafts. The compliments are obviously great, but listen to what everyone says. Try to work out if they have a point and, if they do, work out a solution. Remember that criticism, like praise, is just information, so listen to everything. You are a sponge; take it all in.

Use your senses

There's a reason why people go to markets and food halls rather than restaurants. And it's not just the price, otherwise they'd be having a sandwich. People come to be entertained and impressed, they want to be part of something bigger, cooler and more exciting than the supermarket queue. Appeal to all their senses. Use bright colours, tasty smells, skilled and charming staff, and have cool music playing. Give people the whole experience.

The best thing for your stall is a crowd. A crowd brings people in and makes it feel like more than just lunch. Give them theatre: let them see what you're doing, show off your skills. Don't turn away from them and prepare everything at the back of a dark gazebo. It makes them suspicious and, quite frankly, bored. Give them something to put on their Instagram stories. Not only does it make them look cool, it's effortless, free marketing for you – a win-win. The more interesting you make the whole experience, the more likely it is that people will come back week after week. People don't just have a favourite pub because it sells their favourite beer. It's because they like the seats, the fire, the vibe and the barman. Same goes for your business: even if you've only got your customer for five minutes, make them count.

Prep

Dear Lord, *Prep*. This is where people lose their lives. When people who aren't chefs set up a street-food stall one of the main things they don't take into account is the preparation involved. They find themselves elbow-deep in cauli-rice or slow-cooked pork at 3 a.m. and wonder, *How did I get here? Will I ever sleep again?*

'The first idea of BBQ Dreamz was skewers, but we soon realised: Who wants to skewer hundreds of skewers? That's so many man-hours. Especially when you've made one hundred skewers and then just sell to two people. You think: What am I doing? Have you ever had to dump a whole load of skewers in a bin? It just turns it into a black bag colander, complete nightmare.'
Lee and Sinead, BONG BONGS

How long does it take you to make your product? Have you created a nineteen-hour smoked-beef recipe? Are you making pastry cases throughout the night? The sanest street-food traders I know are the ones who have to do barely any prep before they get to the market. At most markets you have to arrive around 9 a.m. to set up to be ready for midday. Use this time. Work out what you can prep on the stall and do it there. If you can prep the majority of your product in under two hours on the stall, then you're closer to having a semblance of a life. You don't want to trade all day, then pack down, wash up, go to the wholesaler, then the bank and *then* have to prep for six hours. Street food is hard work and demands long hours as it is, so don't make it any harder than it needs to be. Work out a way you can make a great product without having to do it through the night, otherwise you'll burn out too quickly.

You may ignore this and reckon that you're fine to put the hours in to make the best product possible. Well, good on you, but think about the future. If you have to spend six hours in a kitchen to make one hundred sales, then you can't possibly scale up to where you need to be for festivals or big events. If you're doing festivals, you'll be stuck in a field somewhere for just under a week, so you need to be able to do your prep *there* rather than in a fully equipped kitchen. How are you going to manage that? And that's just the timing and logistics, never mind the expense. If you're cooking through the night and then selling it on a market all day you need to be making enough money to pay yourself (or whoever it is) for all those extra hours. Even if at the start you're not paying yourself decently for your own time, you still need to think whether, when the times comes that you will be paying yourself or someone else to put in those hours, the business will be able to support it. How many portions do you have to sell to cover food costs, rent and all those extra hours? Is it feasible? Maybe you are cooking while someone else runs the stall – that's extra staff and a kitchen expense too. All these things add up. Work out how to streamline your business from the outset.

Talk about who, what, how and where
Who are the public – these people you're probably imagining selling to? What are they going to want? A full meal or a snack? How much money do they have? Where are they?

Different strokes for different folks and all that. Work out who your target audience is and choose events based on that. Your food is not going to be successful everywhere, you need to be aware of that and work out if it means you need to change your product or just pick events carefully.

Always remember, people like what they know. It will kill small parts of your soul as you watch people queue to pay £8 for a frozen burger and wholesale sauce, or for a pile of paella which literally just came out of the pack into the pan. All the while you're standing there having made everything from scratch and having practically invented an entirely new food group. However hard it is, you've just got to let it wash over you. No matter where they are, burger stalls will almost always be the busiest stall – there are very few exceptions to this rule. Wraps will always do well at lunch. Paella, vaguely fluorescent noodles, and German sausages will do well at large-scale events and festivals because people are hungover and they want stodge, comfort food and/or the most food for the lowest price. This is slowly changing with the rise in veganism and people eating more healthily, but it is something to keep in mind. If you don't want to compete with these kinds of stall, choose festivals and events wisely. If you're happy to compete, go ahead: people will come, that's clear from the amazing variety across the festival circuit now, but you need to consider how you are going to manage to compete. Smaller festivals can be amazing for street food when they get the ratio of stalls to people right. Some dance festivals, however, are not so good; more often than not you will sell loads of bottles of water and not much else. Maybe some comfort chips the morning after. Dance festivals are not the place for your pea foam.

---

*'For festivals you need to have a feel for the kind of
people who are going to be there and the kind of food*

they might want. We felt comfortable with Latitude because there are a lot of families who are there to eat. I've heard horror stories of people at dance festivals where no one is eating.'

Lisa, Yum Bun

Sometimes some products just don't work on the street. For whatever reason, whether it's because people aren't in the right mood, it's too expensive, too small, too messy or just not in the right place. It's heartbreaking, but you've got to be flexible and keep learning all the time. I know people who have been in the street-food game for five or six years, and we still have conversations about what works where and if it truly works well enough to make a living from it. You can become slightly deranged trying to trick people into eating your food.

'The thing I loved about tacos is that you can have three individual meals, you can completely customise them. But it just didn't work in a street-food setting in London. They're too small, people don't know how to eat them, people don't see them as a meal, they want something in their hand that isn't too messy to eat. One of the first things I had to overcome was doing burritos – I couldn't get my head around having a business called Taco Dave and doing burritos. I finally did it in 2018 and they immediately became the majority of the business.'

Dave, Taco Dave

If you want to make thousands of pounds at a festival, work out who is going to that festival and what they might want. Different festivals and events have very different clienteles. So don't just look at the possible numbers of attendees; look at who they are, what they might be doing and how much cash they have to spend. If you work out who your target clientele is early on and only trade at those events, you will save yourself a lot of time, money and heartache.

Who are your suppliers going to be?

And what do your suppliers say about you as a business? When you're thinking about your product you need to work out where you're going to get all your ingredients from. Who are your suppliers going to be? I'm assuming you want your business to be a success, that you want to stand out from the crowd, so therefore you need to research which suppliers are going to help you to do this. It's no good getting your meat off your mate Gary who had it in the back of his van from an unknown source, no matter how cheap it is. You need quality and you need to show what your supply chain is to the Environmental Health Officer (EHO) when they come knocking. You need to prove that you know where it is from, and that the people who sold it to you know where it's from. It needs to be free from contamination, good quality and from a reliable company, so it therefore needs to be from a trusted professional supplier. Your product needs to make business sense too, so do the research to make sure you're getting the best product at the best deal. While you're researching why not make it local and sustainable, ethical and organic? You need to give yourself the best shot possible, so why not make it all the best things from the start? Even more so if you're doing a twist on a classic: do whatever you can to stand out!

Look around you, what do you have to hand? Not just what is plentiful but also what is going to waste? Plenty of great businesses have created a solution for food which would otherwise just be waste. Look at Marmite for instance, a global brand which is a by-product of beer, and I think we can all agree that they've done pretty well.

'When Dad started the farm, he sold raw meat that was produced on the farm on markets as a way of paying the mortgage. Once he'd got into the meat business in a bigger way he realised that there was much more demand for high-end cuts – such as fillet and sirloin – and not much demand for the stewing cuts – the trim – which is what you can make burgers out of. Now, we're a fully integrated business because making the burgers out of the trim and selling those as street food has allowed us to do more whole carcass butchery. The farm couldn't exist without the street food, it's an essential part of the business, it's high-risk, but the margins are much better than anything else we could do; margins on raw meat are tiny.'

LEO, NORTHFIELD FARM

'Most of the fish was leaving Ullapool and we wanted to keep some of it here. We knew we didn't want to do a

restaurant because it was too much of a risk with all the overheads, so we came up with the catering trailer. We get our catch every day from the local fishermen and we create a menu from what we get in the morning, so that can be anything: lobsters, trout, langoustines, crab or white fish. We just both loved the sea and fishing, so wanted to make the best use of the produce on our doorstep.'

Fenella and Kirsty, THE SEAFOOD SHACK

Stand out from the crowd

If there's something that you're passionate about, find a way to incorporate it into your business. You've found yourself ready to start a business, so you're already thinking outside the box. Go further. There are a million food businesses out there already, so if you have something else you're passionate about see if it will help you stand out. From focusing on your carbon footprint to having amazing music on your stall and music recommendations on Twitter, experiment to see if it makes the business more interesting as a destination. You don't just have to stop at the food; the whole vibe is important in street food. People come for the full experience, and anything that has the scope to widen your audience and make you stand out is a good thing.

Social causes are a great place to start. If you really care about sustainable living, make that the centre of your business and shout about it. Work with charities, help people in the community, organise to drop off any left-over food to a homeless shelter. You don't have to run the business purely focusing on the bottom line, look at the recent surge in B-

Corp certified businesses. These businesses have a triple bottom line ensuring that people, planet and profit all have equal importance. With issues such as rising inequality and the climate crisis as urgent as ever, it's vital that we all take a step back and reassess what success actually looks like now. Setting up a business is already hard, and you may think it will be easier to get the books to balance by buying the cheaper cuts of meat or single-use plastic containers, but it's precisely at this time that you can set the standards for the future. Being eco-friendly can actually save you money in the long run. If you're going to employ people, why not employ those really in need? As we all wake up to the climate crisis lots of events and festivals are now only taking on traders who can prove their sustainability credentials, so you need to think about this from the very beginning. Sustainability is now a necessity rather than a USP.

'Now, after Coronavirus, people will be looking at what a business is about, so don't just be led by profits, look at what impact you can make for your community. The more social conscience in your business from day one the better; customers love it and you're doing good. Businesses need integrity, so don't just say you're giving ten meals to the NHS; customers can see through that. Do more and do it consistently. Customers will come and your profit will come. We are always trying to find a way to do things that aren't just about profit, without being fucking Bono.'

Manjit and Michael, MANJIT'S KITCHEN

Social mobility, the gender pay gap and environmental change are all things that the government should be doing more to change, but it takes them a long time to facilitate any real change. We can all start changing things tomorrow. Big businesses are often too entrenched in the way they do things, but small businesses and start-ups have the freedom to try stuff, throw out the rulebook and start again. If a whole new generation of businesses started to run things differently, then there's the possibility it could create real change within the industry, if not the world (without being fucking Bono).

PRODUCT KEY POINTS

- Do some research.

- Think about the making process.

- Who, what, how and where.

- Stand out from the crowd.

Chapter 3

What is your brand?

Many people think that, in the grand scheme of things, branding isn't that important as the food should speak for itself. They're just wrong. When you're walking round a busy market or festival and trying to work out what to eat, the thing that will pull you in from afar is the branding. A name may make you laugh, or the van would look great on someone's Instagram feed, or the logo reminds you of something from your childhood. Whatever it is, it's the branding that provides the initial impression, communicates who you are and brings you close enough to read the menu, smell the food and see the drama. Good branding is what makes people walk across the street to see what's going on. Especially now, in the age of social media, absolutely everything has to be aesthetically pleasing. If you want to do fancy events and private parties you've got to look the part, something the guests can share on social media to prove how cool they are to their friends. It baffles me when I go into some cafés and restaurants and there's no discernible branding or theme. Branding creates value. This is one of the main aspects that will make you stand out and make people come back, so put your mission on your menu, make it clear who you are and what you're doing.

Otherwise you will just fade into obscurity. There's so much competition out there; give everything you've got, give people more to remember you by.

Name

The best names all have something vaguely related to what they're selling. Don't just use your name unless it naturally suits your brand. If it doesn't suit your brand, it won't work as it doesn't explain anything, and on applications it will just look like you read the question wrong. Choose something short, easy to spell and check that no one else is called it.

Play around with a few different ideas, put it to your friends, have a solid think about it and then leave it and go and do something completely different for a bit. Often, it'll suddenly come to you when you're not thinking of it at all, your brain just spits it out and suddenly you'll think, *Yes, obviously that. I'm a genius.*

Be clear about who you are as a business. If you don't have a big marketing budget, your name needs to do a lot of the legwork for you. People need to read it and know what to expect. When they see you on a line-up for a market or festival, ideally you want the name to give them an idea (at least vaguely) of what the business is about before they've seen the set-up or the food.

Once you've worked out what it is, get the social media handles and buy the website domain name; snap that shit up early on.

If you try to do this and realise they're not available, go back to the drawing board, start again. No one wants to follow '@honest_burger_london743' – it's messy and unprofessional – they want '@honestburger'.

Look

Your name may have already given you an insight into what your 'look' might be. Be it 80s Miami, tropical paradise, Scandi chic, or British bunting, make sure it encompasses your whole stall. You can't have a lovely wooden set-up and then a bog-standard whiteboard menu just clipped on the side. Make it consistent throughout your whole stall. Have a plan before you start buying stuff for the stall so that it matches your 'look' and if you change your 'look' do it all at once, otherwise you have a stall that looks like a second-hand shop of random old failed ideas. No one wants to go there.

Clarity is key, and this is where your business plan comes into play. How and why did you start? What's your mission? All of these things should come into play when planning your look. Show that you care about these things because if you don't care then no one else is going to.

Don't be fooled into thinking everyone has to have a neon sign or an old Citroen van. There's space for all styles; street food is about variety and authenticity, so it wouldn't make sense for us to be cookie-cutter versions of each other. Work out what is authentic for you and your business's vision.

'If I look back on Toastits, I was so young. I was asked at one point, Do I want to be part of this innovative street food with neon lights and fast-moving products, or do I want to be part of the yummy mummy artisan chalkboard scene? At the time I was inexperienced and young, so I was pushed in the wrong direction and ultimately it led to the end of my business. I should have stuck to what I knew my brand was because no one knows the brand better than yourself.'

Philippa, TOASTITS

Logo

A decent logo can make you look a whole lot more professional than you actually are. This is especially important when applying to big events or private gigs. Play around with your name, have a look at logos you like and draw inspiration from them. It doesn't have to be complicated – in fact the general rule is the simpler the better – but it does need to incorporate your name and your look. Getting nowhere? Ask an arty friend for help, play around with some apps. As I said, it really doesn't have to be complicated to start off with. Don't spend loads of money on getting it professionally done at the start, because who you are or what you sell may change dramatically within the first six months. Once you've been up and running for a while and know who you are as a business, then get a freelance designer to do a sexy one for you. Before that, grab a pen and paper and play around.

One of the best pieces of advice I got when trying to figure out a fit-out for a potential restaurant was if you have an idea but you're not sure it'll work, buy cheap versions of what you ultimately want and give it a go. If it doesn't work, then you've not invested loads of money in something that doesn't work or that you hate. If it does work, you can use it until it breaks or until you have the money to upgrade it to the fancier version. This is perfect advice for your branding at the start. Particularly in the first six months your idea of what works and who you are as a business will change a lot, so don't invest loads at the start; play around, ask for help, and do stuff relatively cheaply. Once you know better what works and what doesn't, *that's* the time you can invest in the huge neon sign or the branded gazebo.

Branding is how people perceive the business, so clarity and consistency are key. Use everything: if you're doing something special, shout about it so people know what you stand for, put your message on your menu. While we're on menus, menu items need names – make them interesting, informative or funny, perhaps with a pun. Stand out from the crowd. If this is your signature dish, doesn't it deserve a name?

Authenticity
People come to street food for the authenticity. People love the underdog story of someone selling the best food in town out of a gazebo. For people to believe your story you need to have that integrity and authenticity, otherwise it's just noise. There's a tendency to throw loads of money at an idea to make it work.

42

The charm of street food lies in its slightly rough-around-the-edges nature, so if you turn up on day one with slick corporate branding, people won't buy into you or your business as an underdog story.

'I've lost tens of thousands of pounds by getting the branding wrong in London. We were always just farmers selling burgers on the market and we had everything written on blackboards by hand and then I got rid of the chalkboards and rebranded the whole stall with slick smart signs and it completely destroyed our business for a while. People come with an expectation of what they want, and when they're coming onto a market they want authenticity, they don't want something too polished or perfect. I had spent loads of money getting these smart signs made and we just looked too corporate, no one believed that we were just farmers any more. We went back to the blackboards and sales instantly went back up.'

Leo, NORTHFIELD FARM

If you've got your mission all over your menu and Instagram, then you actually have to abide by it too. Don't lie, people will see through it. Authenticity is key. If it doesn't feel authentic, then *don't do it.*

BRANDING KEY POINTS

Your brand needs to be:

- Clear.

- Concise.

- Authentic.

Chapter 4

Where will you sell it?

Street food encompasses so many things: markets, festivals, events, parties, office catering – and they can all lead to huge opportunities.

Each location has positives and negatives, and each location affects your day-to-day life differently. So how do you want the business to fit into your life? Do you want it to take it over completely en route to a global empire? Or do you want it to be a lifestyle business? Depending on what you want out of your business, there are plenty of options for everybody.

Firstly, this isn't America; you can't just pull up on the street and start trading there, so get that out of your head – again, you're not in *Chef*. Street trading is controlled very strictly in the UK. Because it's very hard to get a street trading licence from the local authority, it is much easier to set up within an established spot. This is especially true in cities and towns. In rural areas regulations seem to be slightly more lenient, but always check with your local council and the landowner first.

We've set up on streets, on rooftops and in fields. In grimy underground stations, fancy offices with ping-pong tables, beside a Roman amphitheatre, in schoolyards and in an outdoor cinema. There are myriad options out there, you just need to figure out which works best for you and your brand.

Where do you want to sell? What is your food? If you're selling crumpets or juices, then a late-night venue probably isn't the right place for you. Where is your target audience? How can you get to them? Will you sell enough to make any money? Will you have to do a combination of markets and events to make decent money? Does it look good enough for people to want to buy? If you are busy, are you organised enough to cope with it?

And remember: 'Everywhere you go, always take the weather with you'. Don't underestimate the power of the weather, and keep it in mind for every event.

Clarity is key

When applying for a spot at any of the following options, what you do and what you are offering needs to be clear. You need to have a one-line answer to what your business does – this is all part of the elevator pitch in your business plan. If you're still rambling on about it after ten minutes, saying, 'Well, you know, it's my authenticity mixed with the culture I absorb and we just see what the flavours are at the end. I don't like to be defined by labels, I just cook what inspires me, let me speak my truth through the flavours and if you don't understand this then you're the idiot, not me, get out of my way'. BORE OFF, MATE. If you want to get onto markets, into festivals and get booked for events, people need to know what you're doing so they can reliably tell others what to expect. You're trying to sell a product here and I'm fairly sure you want return customers. Those customers need to be able to come back and buy that product again and know that it will be exactly the same as last time. That's part of the skill – *dependability*.

Working out what your sales pitch is should be dead easy in street food because you should be focusing on one product so that *it* is the sales pitch. For catering and events you can be more vague, but you still need a line like 'traditional English cooking with a twist', 'Indian feasts', 'vegan junk food'. These descriptions all leave scope for you to do a lot of different things, but the customer still has a pretty good idea of what to expect. When we got married I spoke to several different caterers, one of whom thought they were far too cool for school to do the basic sales pitch and instead called me into his van and told me, 'Yeah, I'll think about the menu closer to the time. I like to keep things spontaneous and free-flowing, you know? I like to cook things with smoke and fire and don't like a kitchen to constrain me, you know?' WHAT EVEN IS THAT? Who are you and what are you saying? Do you understand what words mean? Some people like that kind of thing – to just go with the flow – but the majority of the population like to have a plan and answers for the seventeen thousand questions they get asked by guests when they get married, one of which near the top of the list is 'What are we eating?'.

Feel free to talk like that in a restaurant – people can choose to come to you. Doing it as part of a street-food business is tricky because you've got to apply for that pitch by telling them what you're going to do, so you can't just 'let the spirits guide you' the night before.

Imagine you're deciding what to eat and one place is really clear about what is on offer and is pretty slick about getting it out; and then next door there's a stall where everything is slow and a bit all over the place because they've not streamlined their offering, and it's not clear what they're actually offering because their branding no longer matches the menu. I know which one I'd choose. Success in street food is essentially down to practice and repetition: getting to a point where you can get one hundred portions of perfectly cooked, Instagrammable food out in an hour is a skill. Don't knock it.

Being clear gives people the safety they need to experiment. They're on the street, so a lot of the 'safe' factors have gone out of the window. What encourages them to actually eat something is that you're an expert at this one thing, so you'll look after them. Make it clear and make them feel like they're in the hands of an expert. The product itself can be as mad as you like, just make sure you're clear about what it is and how to get it out.

> *'One of the first events we did I wrote the whole menu in Welsh and then in brackets had the date of the original recipe, but people were just like "What the hell is that?". So I learnt that I had to be clear quite quickly.'*
>
> Alex, PINK PEPPERCORN

Okay, enough of all of that. Here are the obvious trading options.

Markets

Weekly, monthly, daily, whatever it is they're generally pretty regular and year-round. These are your bread and butter, especially at the start. Location, marketing and weather can all play a part in whether they're any good or not. Sometimes you strike gold and other times you end up in the mud. You live and learn. As you go on you will work out what looks and sounds like a good market and what doesn't. Due to the huge boom in street food there's now a (smaller) boom of people setting up markets. Many are excellent, and run by knowledgeable, fair people. Others are less so and run by people who appear not to have any idea what's going on and are charging obscene rents. Keep an eye out, ask around, go and visit a market when it's on. Get the lie of the land, if you can, before you start handing over money. There's a huge variety of markets out there now and each have their benefits. Work out which is the best for you and your brand. Look at the other traders too – are you happy to be associated with them? Would you eat there? Are your customers there? We can't all be going to neon-signed markets with banging music; sometimes you want to go to a farmers' market, sometimes a weekday market – they all have their place.

Pros

- Regular spot = regular income.

- An excellent way to build up a regular customer base.

- You get to try things out, and get real feedback each week.

- You can start to analyse trends based on date, weather and location. This will help you get better at stock control. Better stock control = better profits.

- A great place to work out who you are as a brand and get used to the ins and outs of running a business. Cheaper rents and shorter days mean you have space to mess up, improve and develop, which you certainly don't get at festivals or events.

Cons
- Depending on where it is, your output is likely to be smaller compared to festivals and events.

- Markets will want your attendance throughout the year, so you have to be prepared to be there every day/week/month, otherwise they'll find someone who is.

How to apply
Every market has its own website. If you can't for the life of you find that they'll have a social media page. That will have links to the page or contact details for new applicants. Look through it all carefully, make sure you follow the instructions on how to apply and don't just send them a private message without doing what they ask you to first. The application form is there for a

reason; you're not going to endear yourself to the manager of the market if you can't follow the basic instructions on how to apply. Don't ask other traders to get you in without having done the basic application first. Feel free to do this once you have applied properly, then you can pull out all the stops: send a private message, see if someone can put in a good word for you, but just make sure you've covered the basics first. For popular markets there is often a long waiting list and fierce competition, so persistence is key. Keep improving and applying, be available, and be reliable when they offer you a trial.

'I had quite a few steady, good markets, so it made it much easier to plan for the future and work out how to grow. Then we could buy two sets of equipment to double up on at weekends. We never went down the festival route because we had a decent weekly income from the regular markets. The key to success was just commitment: we turned up every single Saturday and Sunday, rain or shine, which was why I got the good pitches in the first place. I quite liked the routine. And it's good training for if you do open a restaurant one day; you've got to be open every day, otherwise you lose customers.'

Carol, DEENEY'S

Festivals

Oh so much fun: all summer spent in fields across the country having a wild time. Work all summer and chill all winter – why not? There are great festivals out there, but you've got to find the right ones for your product and make sure your logistics are on point. Think about how you would behave if you were a customer. How much food would you eat and how often? Look at how many traders there are and how long the event is. If it's a gig bear in mind people will eat before or after, so you need to make your money in that short amount of time. Are you quick enough?

Pros

- Has the potential to make more money than other options: so many people, stuck in a field for a long time, they've got to eat.

- Can be good publicity and a badge of honour to show that you can scale up.

- So much fun! Customers are generally in a really good mood and are often wearing ridiculous outfits. There's music all the time and a seemingly never-ending stream of beer and parties to go to when you finally close. It's hard work, but certainly doesn't feel like it.

- Excellent marketing opportunity. Festivals get your name out to a wider audience, opening up many potential streams of revenue. You never know who might come to your stall and offer you an amazing opportunity.

Cons

- Higher rents.

- Extra costs: travel for everyone to get there, staff for however many days you need them. How are you going to keep your food fresh? Do you need to hire a refrigerated van? Do you have enough equipment? Is the equipment big enough to get the portions out you need? All these things add up.

- Logistics are more complicated: How are you going to get there? How are all the staff going to get there? Where are they going to sleep? Have you got stuff to sleep in? Are they going to be reliable after a big night? When do you have to be there? Generally, the organisers will want you there two or three days before the site opens, at a minimum. How does this work with your other festivals? Are they back-to-back?

- Long hours, and I mean *long*. Depending on the festival and where you are located you could be working nonstop for pretty much 20 hours – those queues just won't go down. Getting to enjoy any of the festival is a bonus rather than a given.

- Stock: How much are you going to take? Will it last? Can your suppliers deliver to wherever you are, will they be allowed on site? Is there somewhere nearby you can get stock from?

- The weather, your location within site and your actual opening hours: you need to take into account all these things. We've had days cancelled due to bad weather and a whole festival closed down with no recompense. Traders arriving and realising they've been placed in a field which doesn't open until 4pm. Some being promised an amazing spot and instead being put in the corner of a field miles from anyone, others being so far away from running water it meant that they were never able to keep prep up with demand. These are worst-case scenarios, but a possibility for everyone. Make sure you have as much information as possible. Check the contracts, make sure it is clear what you are getting and what you expect for your money – this is a business transaction after all. Have a look at your insurance, see if you can get cover for early closures, extreme weather, cancellations, etc. Don't get caught out because you didn't read all the information thoroughly.

How to apply

Food at festivals is generally run by big agencies that are subcontracted to find, organise and manage all the traders on site. This is how you get in: find the agencies, make sure you're on their books and then, when they send you the festival options, apply to whichever you fancy. Some festivals still organise food traders in-house, so if you have specific ones in mind, it's worth doing research early on to work out if that's the case and who you need to get in touch with.

Festivals also get organised earlier than you might think, with people generally sending off heaps of applications between October and December to find out from January onwards where they'll be trading (or not) in the summer. So, if in April you suddenly fancy trading at a big festival, you're too late. Likewise for Christmas festivals and events: the big popular ones are generally organised and booked up by August at the very latest.

If you're looking at smaller local events and festivals, get in touch with your local tourist information, find local events lists, buy the events directory and get in touch with the people who run them. Good relationships with these people are vital: be charming and organised.

'At the start we tried everything to see what worked. Some people are good at markets, others at festivals or private events, but it just depends on your lifestyle and what you like. We ended up doing festivals because we were into festivals when we first started, it suited our food and we hated setting up and packing down for just a few hours. We still needed to do some private events though because festivals can be so risky.'

Anna and Tony, ANNA MAE'S

Indoor market halls

Popping up all over the country, these are the new hubs for foodies. Why go to a restaurant where you all have to eat the same thing, when you can have all the variety and excitement of street food with none of the weather and you can sit on a sofa, with a table for your food and beer out of a real glass? So much more civilised. Indoor market halls are the sweet spot between a restaurant and a market. They are a great place to work out if you really want to take the next step up to opening a restaurant.

Pros
- They are generally in a very central location, or at least are a destination in themselves.

- You are now part of a bigger and more experienced operation, and this can help you raise your game. The organisers should provide health and safety support, maintenance, and their marketing will reach a much wider audience than you would have managed alone.

- They are not reliant on weather.

- They generally run seven days a week, so excellent for stock control and a steady flow of money.

- You don't have to set up and pack down every day.

Cons
- They are a bigger operation, so require a bigger outlay, cost-wise. This is a proper kitchen you have

to equip, with an extraction fan, rather than just a few bits in a gazebo.

- You'll be contracted for a certain amount of time, which is bad if it's not a popular destination. Do your research, go and sit there at different times to check that there's the footfall before you sign your life away.

- You need to be a slick operation, so this is not a place to start off. You need to be able to provide high-quality, delicious food while keeping your health and safety standards top-notch. You'll need a team of staff and clear protocols in place. This is not a place for you to 'try things out' and make mistakes. Get your practice in beforehand.

- They carry bigger overheads: business rates often apply, as does a service charge to keep the site running and clean.

How to apply

There are opportunities across the country – you just have to find them and apply via the websites. If you're interested in street food you probably already know the ones in your area. Indoor market halls have limited space and tend to be busy, so obviously they're hugely popular and have long waiting lists. If you're a member of the Nationwide Caterers Association (NCASS – more on this later) you may also receive notifications if there's a chance of a guest-spot in certain locations. Because of the popularity of market halls persistence is key. Experience and popularity are what the managers of the halls are looking for, so up your Instagram and Twitter campaigns, show them how great you are and how many people will come to their market hall if you are a permanent fixture. This will help your application immeasurably, so look further afield and get as many big-profile events under your belt first. So just quality food, quality branding and a quality following. Easy, eh?

'I always thought [Yum Bun] suited being a small takeaway concept, and in the past few years there's been loads of interest in food halls, so we've made ourselves really well placed to expand in those places. I can't pretend that that was ever the major grand plan; it's just been as opportunities come along you weigh up what feels right and what makes sense.'

Lisa, YUM BUN

Private events

Birthdays, weddings, Christmas parties. Due to the rise of quality food coming from the street-food scene people are keen to cash in on the 'cool factor' and have you at their event. It's definitely more interesting than a cold buffet with soggy sausage rolls. Often, it'll just be you there and it should be pre-paid. Many traders see these as the holy grail of gigs, but you've got to take everything into account.

Pros

- There is very little risk involved as you are paid upfront for a certain number of portions.

- They are easy to prep and order for because you know exactly how many servings you will sell.

- They are not reliant on the weather.

- Your clients have paid for that food, so they'll have it no matter what.

- It's an amazing marketing opportunity if you look good and do a good job. Everyone at the event has the chance to see you in action and be so impressed by you that they might book you themselves. Bring your 'A' game.

Cons

- This is someone's big event, therefore you've got to be completely on it. No messing around, you can't run out of food, turn up late or forget anything. There is nowhere to hide shoddy organisation at private events.

- Often everyone will want to eat at the same time, so you need to be able to cope with high volume at speed.

- Your set-up has to be top-notch. People are paying to have you as part of their big day, so you can't just show up with your second-best gazebo and a handwritten sign. You're there to make them look good. Make sure you do.

- You often have to expand your menu to accommodate everyone. That can include vegan, meat- or gluten-free options. If you are against giving people choice this may pain you, but it's the name of the game when it comes to private events.

How to apply

There are many agencies out there that specialise in wedding catering or private events. You just need to find them and get on their database. If it's something you're keen on doing, make sure you have it clearly on your website and social media too, this way fans of yours know that you're a viable option for that big birthday bash and event agencies will get in touch too.

Private venues will generally use the same caterers again and again because they don't need to go out and look for new ones. To get in with them you need to get your hustle on, do some face-to-face meetings, bring food with you, get experience in less popular venues to show you can cope – start small and build up.

'Our signature dish came from a young Indian couple who wanted me to do Punjabi Indian food for their wedding. She loved masala dosas, so asked if I could make

them. I told her I could but that mine are very different from the south Indian ones that everyone is familiar with. The ones I make are from a recipe given to me by a guy I saw making them once when I was fourteen years old, who then disappeared off the face of the earth! Even the people in his village don't know where he went. It was as though he was meant to be in my life and it's his masala dosas that have inspired mine. I did that wedding and then the word just spread, the dosas became the talk of the Asian community around the Sussex area, we were then nominated for several awards and the business just escalated from there, all from just one wedding.'

Ranie, JAH JYOT

Office catering

You know the fancy offices with the ping-pong tables and an office dog? The ones you think only exist in films? These guys want you. They love giving their staff choice and treats. Bringing you into their office every lunchtime is the cool version of having a canteen. Plus, if you go to them, then they don't have to go anywhere, so their employees *never leave*.

Pros

- It's not reliant on the weather as you will usually be inside, or close enough for it not to matter.

- You get, generally speaking, a captive audience, possibly with very limited alternatives, depending on where the office is.

- It can provide regular, reliable income, depending on your relationship and popularity with the clientele; and bigger profit margins if you do the same office each week, as you'll get to know roughly how many portions you can take.

- Sometimes pre-paid or subsidised by the company, resulting in less risk and more cash for you.

Cons
- If it is indoors, you'll need a full electric set-up and a product that doesn't create smoke, too strong a smell, or too much mess – in some respects the opposite of what makes a good street-food stall interesting and exciting. It needs to be clean, quiet and leave no trace.

- You often have to expand your menu here to include the vegans, the carnivores and the gluten-free all under one roof.

- Creating relationships with the offices can be difficult. There are various companies out there whose sole job is to organise this stuff. You need to get into their good books and stay in them.

How to apply
The easiest way is through an agent who has already built up the relationship with the client and knows (roughly) how many

portions you need to do, dietary requirements and office rules. As always, find these agents, get on their books and go from there.

If you're savvy and have connections, then you can try to set up a connection on your own. Office managers and social executives are always looking at ways to bring their staff together, so if you have a link with one use it, because the worst thing they can say is no.

'The office catering is what has made me the biggest profit, which has then given me the money to save and get into a more permanent site. Office catering is the best place for margins because you're doing most of it at home with fewer staff. So although it can be stressful because you're working with a lot of different people with a lot of different needs and sometimes the customers don't appreciate the food or the work you've put in, it can be such a good earner. It's the closest thing to getting a dependable wage as you can get rather than just hoping for the best. With office catering you can plan ahead and depend on the money pretty consistently.'

Alastair, TEMAKI BROS

Pop-ups

If your aim is to one day get into a bricks-and-mortar premises, then this can be a fantastic way to try it out without signing your life away. There are a multitude of options out there for you. Pubs are one: many have realised that rather than employing, organising and managing a kitchen of their own, they can get in a rotation of interesting street-food traders to use the facilities they already have. Other people's failed businesses are another: there is a high turnover of businesses trying and failing, with people finding themselves stuck with long leases on units they can't afford. This may be particularly prevalent after Covid-19. You can find these units and rent them for short periods of time and so see if your idea works without so much of the risk.

Pros
- Once you're in you're in: there's no set-up and pack-down each day.

- If you're in a pub you've already got a captive audience. If the pub has a track record of pop-ups, it should be pretty easy to work out stock and staff.

- If your aim is a permanent unit, then the experience of popping up in one will be an excellent selling point to any potential unit landlord.

- Great in the winter as pop-ups are not dependent on the weather.

Cons
- It can be quite an expensive experiment if it doesn't go well. It's essential you do the maths before you hand over any money.

- As always with new spots, it can take time to drum up business. If you've only got the spot for three weeks, then you need to make sure that your marketing is on point so people know you're there.

- Check the licence: are you legally allowed to cook in there? You need an A3 or A5 licence for hot food, so don't sign up to something you can't actually use.

How to apply

For pop-up units there are agencies out there who clear pricing deals with the landlords directly. 'Appear Here' is a fantastic one with a multitude of options and, more often than not, if you can't find what you're looking for they will point you in the right direction. It is much safer, when doing a pop-up, to do it through an agency as they deal with all the legal stuff to do with the lease of the building itself, what you're allowed to do, etc. You don't want to hand over three weeks' worth of rent to a family friend who has a shop standing empty to find that it's only a week in and you're being turfed out because they've ignored their leasing restrictions.

For pubs it's worth doing research in your local area. For your first one it's best to go with a pub that has a track record of doing pop-ups, that way you know there's at least a market for it and they (should be) more organised than those who haven't rented out their kitchen before. To find those that already do it, search online and on Instagram. One of the most useful aspects of Instagram is that you can follow traders in the same city as you, and you can see where they are and what they're doing. So if you see them popping up in a cool place or a pub, then it shows it's possible. Do some research and get in touch with the place or pub first, don't just message the trader asking how they got in there. They will generally help, but it's really annoying when people who haven't even tried to do it off their own bat first ask you for a leg up (it's clear when this is the case, particularly when the application process is blindingly obvious, and it will not make you many friends). Just do the work.

'I had jumped head-first into this and had no other income, so I needed to look at ways to earn more and look for facilities to do that because I couldn't just cook from home. Always look for an opportunity that is right in front of you. My local pub used their kitchen but not all the time, so I did a deal with them where I didn't have to pay rent to use their kitchen; my rent was me working one or two shifts behind the bar. So, I'd do all my prep in the kitchen, had all my equipment there, got the kitchen checked over by an Environmental Health Officer and then did my two shifts as payment. It evolved from there because I could talk to locals about what we were doing, so I managed to get pre-orders in for the market. Then it started to take off, so I suggested to the pub I do a curry night once a week. They agreed and the first one was sold out – about 70 covers. Word got out, the local curry club came down at the next one and gave me a standing

ovation. That was the turning point. We didn't have to spend a lot of money; it was down to being imaginative and creative about the way we approach situations.'

Ranie, JAH JYOT

Keep an open mind

Once you're more established, if you see a good location and nothing has been set up there yet, find the person who owns it and ask. The worst that could happen is that they say no. Think outside the box.

Don't be fooled by the big famous events; they are great but not necessarily the biggest money-makers. Local events can be as, if not more, profitable. And don't knock the weekly spots either – they might not be as exciting or glamorous as the festivals and events but there's a lot to be said for dependable year-round income. Don't be frustrated if it takes you a while to find where your product works; you will find it, and you'll learn a whole lot along the way.

'By our second summer I had quit my job and we did everywhere and everything and, actually, we lost money, especially on the weekday markets. We worked out festivals weren't a safe bet for our product too, they were only going to be good if it was a heatwave, so that was too much of a gamble. By the third summer we had rethought things and managed to fine-tune the business; we were then making more money and I wasn't killing myself for it. I think we needed to go

through the rough patch, though, because without that
we wouldn't have found where our product worked.'
Sophia, NONNA'S GELATO

If you are a member of NCASS (more on that later) they will also send you work opportunities. These encompass a whole range of events and can be a fantastic lifeline for those starting out without many other options, and once you have done a few you start to become part of a network of traders, which is so vital when finding trading spots.

All organisers want is for things to go smoothly. They want happy attendees, who are happy if the food is delicious and reasonably priced. If you're behaving badly or have given the event organiser untold stress by emailing them with pointless questions and then being rude to people on the day, then it doesn't matter how good your food is, you will not be asked back.

As in life, don't put all your eggs in one basket. To be a success you need to have a few different sources of income. That way if something goes tits up then you know you've got money coming in from somewhere. Look at big businesses – they don't just have one client. See the festival company you work for as one client, see the market you do as another, and that Christmas market you do as yet another. You need to have a range of revenue streams, so that if something happens to one of them then you're still okay. Just think about the worst-case scenario: if the market you're trading at is privately owned, they could go bust or just stop doing it at any time, or you might get pushed out of it. Whatever it is, you need to have a safety net. It might rain all summer, so your markets have been shit, but it's okay because you've also had a few pre-paid private events in the diary. Your weekly spot is suddenly cancelled because another market has come in and tripled the price, or, I don't know, there might be a worldwide epidemic and the whole country is in lockdown, but you're okay because you do takeaway from a private kitchen. Who knows what might happen. When your payslip is dependent on the weather, world events and people being able to go outside it's useful to have as many revenue streams open as possible.

'Street food is really hard in regional areas because there's not really a town where you can do it. We've seen a lot of people come and go; a lot of people are still going for it but there were three or four evenings a week where we were in small villages or beachside, which sounds very idyllic, but in reality if the weather's rubbish then absolutely no one will come. And because we didn't have a space where we were working from constantly, we didn't have people who knew where we'd be, so couldn't really build up a customer base. That's why the business diversified and we started doing pop-ups and private catering because then we knew where we'd be, how many people [we would need], how much money it would cost us, so there wasn't so much unpredictability. When we realised that festivals were taking us away from home a lot and we weren't actually making that much money *from them we went more into private catering. It's much more of a known quantity: you can limit waste, you know how much you need, and from a cashflow point of view we're taking deposits in January for summer weddings, which helps us pay for things when generally in the winter cashflow is quite lean.'*

Beth and Jim, SEADOG

You've got to decide what is best for you and make the lifestyle work for you. The busiest markets and events are often on evenings and at weekends. If this is going to do your head in, then it's probably not the game for you. The big festivals are throughout the whole of summer; the pop-ups for the World Cup or the Olympics are busiest on the big days, so you will be working rather than being there as a punter. You may want to go into street food so you can be part of these great events but remember, you will be there as a business owner rather than a punter, you'll see it all from a different perspective and have other things on your mind rather than just having a good time. Don't get me wrong, you can still have fun. My most fun working days have, of course, been at festivals – you're working longer and harder than you have before but there's music, people dressed up having fun, and beer. But then you'll have all those distractions while trying to work out if you've broken even and gauge if your mate is too hungover to operate the fryer. Flying-by-the-seat-of-your-pants stuff. And, of course, then you're off when everyone else is back to work. Lots of street-food businesses take the whole of January off because the weather's terrible, no one has any money and people are on fad diets. So while everyone else is trudging through the sleet to work you can be on a month-long holiday on a beach. Not bad, eh?

Before we started we used to have wild nights out and big weekends, but once we set up Shrimpy that all stopped, partly because we really needed to be on top form at work, but mostly due to lack of cash (have I mentioned we were pretty rubbish at the beginning?). We changed our lifestyle for the business; our mate who lived around the corner from the market had us over instead and we drank cheap beer and he listened to us bang on about Shrimpy until the early hours. God knows why he's still our friend. Being able to do that kept us going and meant we didn't give up, but you do have to adapt your life. Don't expect it all just to fit in around it, you'll only resent it.

'Remember it's a lifestyle not just a business. It's not going to make you that rich, so you need to make it work for you – that's what will help you get through the hard times. If you don't make it work you'll just become bitter about it.'

Carol, DEENEY'S

There are so many benefits to street food which aren't money: the freedom, flexibility, creativity, variety, etc, so make it all work for you. If you want to have winter off and just do festivals and events in the summer, then fine: do the maths and make it work. If you want to do weekly office parties and catering, then fine: work out how to do it. Want to be part of someone's routine every Saturday morning? That's also fine. There are so many different roads you can go down as a street-food trader – choose the best for you and make it work.

'I think we all always have the feeling that we should be doing more and that being static isn't very ambitious and I should be looking at more opportunities to grow and expand but honestly, at the moment everything works and we make money. It's very much a lifestyle business at the moment. I have a small child and may have another soon, and the business works around that as it is, which is an achievement in itself. When it comes to the time that I can dedicate everything to it then it will expand, but it works currently and I enjoy it, so what more do you actually want?'

Sophia, NONNA'S GELATO

WHERE TO DO IT KEY POINTS

- There are lots of ways to make money.

- Work out which location works for your food and your brand; not everything is going to work everywhere.

- Which locations work for you and your life?

- Don't put all your eggs in one basket – cover your back.

Chapter 5

How will anyone know about you?

It can be wearing having to think about another aspect of the business, especially one where you don't have any experience. I get it, it can feel impossible trying to keep all the plates spinning but, really, they are all important, and in particular marketing. Marketing is how you tell people who you are and what your aim is. Successful marketing is more about the story you create with your product rather than the product itself. How does the product make people feel, how is it enhancing their day-to-day life? Think about the adverts you see on TV: the ones for coffee aren't really about the coffee, are they? It's about who you have the coffee with, where you have it and, sometimes, whether or not the coffee will get you laid.

People come to street-food markets and events because they are already buying into a story, they're there because they care about grassroots start-ups over faceless chains, so part of the work has already been done for you. You then need to confirm what they're looking for: a small, passionate business with great skills selling great food. But how do you get people from not knowing about you to actually buying your food? You need to do a good D.E.E.D (bear with me . . .):

- **Discover:** They need to find you somewhere, whether it be on social media, on a search engine or on the street. How do they initially get your name in their head?

- **Everywhere:** Once they follow you on social media you need to keep popping up on their feed; there's no point if you do one post a week as you'll get lost in the algorithms. So, you need to be posting regularly about where you are, your product and your story. This is also why lots of street-food businesses do lots of events in the first two years, to get their name out there to as many people as possible so people keep discovering them everywhere.

- **Experience:** They've finally given in after seeing you everywhere and they're going to buy your product. This is when they discover whether you're worth the hype or not. Is the whole experience what you promised it would be on social media?

- **Dependability:** If the customer enjoyed the experience and it was what they expected (and more), they will come back again and again, because they know they can depend on the experience to be consistently good. Hopefully they'll bring new customers too.

You don't need a big budget to do this at all, you just need your phone and your story. Once you're up and running and are keen to invest in a marketing expert, then by all means do it, but you don't need to do it in the first six months; start the work yourself, get some followers and stick to the free stuff. There's a lot you can do with the free stuff.

Social media

Social media is essentially a free billboard on the internet. It does a multitude of jobs: it improves your SEO (Search Engine Optimisation), it can help your customer service, and it's great for building up contacts and finding work. You can follow street-food traders in your area and see where they are trading and work out how you can trade there too.

Due to the transient nature of street food you need to keep people updated about where you actually are so that they know how to find you. Social media is perfect for this as people look at it every day. Sharing content is key to customer loyalty; the fact that you're in different places all the time already gives you plenty to post about.

Advertise your links on your stall and on your packaging, make sure that people know what they are and get them to follow you, encouraging them with discounts for following. To get more followers use hashtags, follow others and post good pics regularly. Even if all of this bores you to death, get in the habit of doing a little bit every day or every other day. It needn't take long, just ten minutes, but once you start posting regularly rather than sporadically, you'll notice the difference.

Instagram

Instagram is an absolute boon when it comes to street food. No one really cares what you have to say, they just want to see tasty pics to salivate over on their commute. Get on it and get set up. If you're no good at taking pictures, there are loads of ways to improve:

- Do some research on the accounts you like and see how they're doing it.

- There are loads of blogs, books or YouTube videos that show you what makes a photo better and how, what tricks you can use. Read these.

- Got a friend who thinks they're a dab hand at Instagram? Ask them if they can come down to the stall one day and take a shedload of pics, then you've got a whole set ready to go.

Decent pictures are essential to getting you spots on markets, any media recognition and, of course, any following on Instagram. You may think that you don't care about how popular you are on Instagram, but if you want to get onto high-profile markets, into food halls and events, then how big your following is on social media is a key component to getting those spots. Market managers want more people to come to their market, so if they have a choice between a trader who has a 300-person reach and one with a 5,000-person reach you can guess who they're going to choose.

A bad picture of your food can do more to put people off than anything else, and it's astonishing how many of these there are. People just take a snap in bad lighting with a bin in the background and think it's fine. Once you start taking pictures you will begin to learn what works and what doesn't; everything takes time and your style will develop, so don't be too hard on yourself at the start. Practice makes perfect. You will also need these pictures when you apply to pretty much any market, festival or event, so make sure you've got at least three you're really proud of, preferably in high-res, otherwise you've no hope.

Same goes with what you write: it's important that you have a 'voice' on social media. Have one person who's in control and let them get on with it. It's confusing if you have two people running it and one leaves really upbeat funny captions while the other writes the bare minimum. Brands have to be consistent, that's why people come back.

Twitter

Twitter is a conversation: to get any decent following you've got to converse with people, retweet things that interest you, respond to other people's tweets, ask the Twitter-sphere questions and see what happens. Stay professional, keep the tweets business- and food-related. Don't go on about how excited you are about getting wasted in the pub or that you're annoyed with Virgin Trains. You wouldn't do this on the business Twitter if it wasn't your business so don't do it now; be professional and be consistent.

'We started off as a home kitchen takeaway service. We wanted to do something together, so we looked at what we had and it was essentially a kitchen, a car and a Twitter account. Twitter had just started at that time. So, the first day we just put out a tweet asking if anyone wanted some home-cooked food delivered to their house and loads of people said yes! So we did that every Friday and Saturday and then quickly outgrew that ... Twitter has been the foundation of our business. Many people say not to bother with it and just use Instagram, but Twitter works for us and our voice because we're more wordy than we are visual. It also enables us to be subversive and lets us take the piss out of things and say things we can't say elsewhere. We have a voice and a tone on Twitter that works for us and we've built that up over time.'

Manjit and Michael, MANJIT'S KITCHEN

Facebook

Facebook pages are funny things. You can post great ads relatively cheaply and people do still seem to use Facebook. However, it does often feel like it's only your auntie and her mates on it, so what's the point? Generally, your auntie and her mates will be coming to your stall anyway, so it's not enticing many new customers. On the other hand, why not use every free platform available? Who knows who you may reach and there are plenty of people who only use Facebook, so without it how would you ever reach them? Plus, you can link up all your accounts on Instagram or on an app called Buffer, so if it doesn't take up any more of your time, why the hell not?

Other cheap marketing options

- **Setting up your own website:** This will instantly make you look more together and a more professional bet. Make sure it has everything on it: your story, social media links, where people can find you, your contact details, and of course some delicious high-resolution pictures. It should be a one-stop-shop for your business info.

- **Set up on 'Google my business':** If you have a fixed daily or weekly spot this makes sure you pop up on people's searches when they're nearby, which improves your local search optimisation massively.

- **Trip Advisor:** Depending on how touristy the spot you're in is, this may not be necessary. However, it is worth setting up a business page as lots of people will look through it for recommendations – why not be part of the pile?

- **Word of mouth:** The better you are, the quicker it will spread. Get people talking about you, be friendly, delicious and well-priced. Easy.

- **Leaflets if you're near a busy hub:** Let people know where you are and what you do! You could combine this with special offers or loyalty cards.

- **Press releases:** You are in a cool interesting industry, so people are keen to cover it. Create a clear, concise press release with some high-resolution pictures to help generate coverage for key moments of growth.

'Because of my background in advertising I knew how to write a press release and had one ready with some high-definition photos. I knew that they wanted a press release explaining who we are, what the product is, what we're trying to do, where and why, so I had something on my phone to send off straight away. Be really responsive to journalists. And learn to prioritise the marketing – it is as important as the product.'

Carol, DEENEY'S

Your shop window

No matter what other marketing you do, your stall will always be your biggest advert, so it needs to be and look top-notch, run smoothly, and *you* need to be charming to customers; you never know who they might be. Years ago, we did a festival that closed halfway through due to bad weather and was quite a hit on our finances. However, one of our customers at that festival was the person who did the marketing for Old Spitalfields Market, where some years later we got a spot in their food hall. We got that spot because she discovered us at that festival, enjoyed the experience and has since been a loyal customer.

'We couldn't have just opened a restaurant and people would have come; the people who do come are the people

who have followed us through street food for ten years. It's been like a ten-year marketing drive through weddings and festivals to get people to want to come to the restaurant. What's (hopefully) going to get us through this Corona thing is the people who are along with us on the journey. The first weekend of lockdown we put up on Twitter that we were doing takeaways from our house again and we ended up having 218 unanswered emails – they were just the ones we couldn't deliver to and didn't even have the time to reply to and say sorry. That shows the following we've managed to build up through street food, which has kept the restaurant going and what will hopefully get us through this.'

Manjit and Michael, MANJIT'S KITCHEN

You need to be dependable and reliable. If people can't find you, then they'll lose interest.

'The first two years we'd go to the festivals and it was so much fun and great for marketing and to get our name out there. But then our regular spot in Ullapool got so much busier with the increase in popularity of the North Coast 500 and tourism in general. You see, the problem with festivals is that you have to travel and be there to set up a day or so early, so for a festival that runs three days, after travel, setting up and packing down you've lost a week of trading. We had a good seven-day-a-week spot and it seemed daft to let that suffer for the odd festival here and there. Especially as if we were away at a festival and customers came to

Ullapool to find us not there – it's really bad for your reputation as a business. It only takes a few people to write on Trip Advisor that we weren't there and that puts others off coming.

Fenella and Kirsty, THE SEAFOOD SHACK

MARKETING KEY POINTS

- Do a good D.E.E.D.

- Find your voice on social media.

- Write a clear press release.

- Remember, your biggest marketing device is your stall, so be consistent and reliable.

Chapter 6

Who will help you?

There are obviously pros and cons to setting up alone or with a partner. If you go it alone, it's all on you, which might be exactly what you want: complete control, no reliance on anyone, but those are also the reasons it makes it harder. You may need someone to share the load physically and emotionally, someone to bounce ideas off and to discuss future projects with. There will be bad days where it's essential to have someone next to you who fully understands quite how bad it's been. You can moan all you like to your boyfriend, girlfriend, best mate or dog, but after a while it will just become wearing to them and to you because they just aren't as invested as you. A business partner will keep you going when you feel like none of it is worth it, and vice versa. On a very basic level, humans need the companionship of someone who understands when you've had a truly terrible day. Someone to talk it through with over a pint or just to stare at a wall with, wondering what to do next. Who that person is is up to you.

Partner

'It's difficult with a romantic partner but also very difficult on your own. I don't know how people do it;

there are so many questions and knockbacks. It can be quite lonely if you do it alone. You learn a lot about each other – it's a massive learning curve. At the beginning we argued a lot, whereas now we're much better and worked out that we need to have split responsibilities and separate areas of expertise. I couldn't do it without her but I'm not sure if I'd recommend it.'

Anna and Tony, ANNA MAE'S

Friend

'It's been really helpful that it's been a partnership throughout the whole thing; I wouldn't have wanted to do it on my own. It's very beneficial that she's not also my life partner because it means we can go away with our own partners and keep the business going. Having two of us also means we can do more than one location at a time without too much stress. You always end up spending more time with people you work with than your family, so it's always going to be a strain, but as a general rule it's worked pretty well. It's a sibling-like relationship; you put up with things that annoy you, but you understand each other as well.'

Beth and Jim, SEADOG

Working in such close quarters with someone, no matter how much you initially liked them, is always going to be hard. Sometimes it works, sometimes it doesn't. The best partnerships I've seen are when people bring different skills to the table. This at least means you both have your own areas of expertise and can focus on those, and if there's anything neither of you know, then you can work it out together. This involves trusting the other person to do a good job, and also working out what is an equal share of the work. Do what you're both good at and divvy up the crappy jobs. Being clear and fair is key.

'We've always had a 50/50 partnership, but when we get paid in the summer we get paid hourly, so there's never any fight about who is working more; it's just really clear. One of us has kids and the other doesn't, so she is obviously available to put more hours in, but it's swings and roundabouts, and sometimes she does more and then it's me. But to keep it fair, our monthly pay is an hourly rate. And to be honest we've been doing that for five years and it's worked. It's because we're on the same wavelength, our drive is the same; we want the business to thrive, we want the fishermen to get what they deserve too, because without the fishermen we wouldn't have the shack, and we want it all to be for the locals and for the community.'

Fenella and Kirsty, THE SEAFOOD SHACK

It's not impossible to do it by yourself: I know loads of people who have done it alone, but it's twice as hard. But on the plus side, you will have more money. Running a partnership does automatically split the profits 50/50, whereas if you're going it alone all that cash is for you. But you'll have to work for it and you need to be across everything. You'll need to be shit-hot at finding staff and managing them, all while keeping everything else afloat. You'll need to be mates with everyone you meet so people will help you when you need it with your stiff gazebo, your heavy fryer, getting a jump-start for your car or just to have someone to moan about the rain with. However, you *can* make it work and relish it.

'I totally love the independence; it is my food, the freedom to do what I want and I get to choose which events to do. If you do it with someone else, you've got to have exactly the same values. I just totally love working for myself, by myself – it's great.'

Alex, PINK PEPPERCORN

Even if you go it alone street food is based on people. You are constantly interacting with people: market managers, other traders, your suppliers, employees and, of course, the customers. You need to be a people person. If the thought of mindless chat with stallholders, long-winded meetings about markets or festivals and negotiating over the phone with suppliers fills you with dread, don't do it. You need to be able to talk to people and not be rude. It will make your life a million times easier if you can find it within you to take your head out of your own arse and chat. Yes, you may think you've created the best burger since the dawn of time, but for God's sake don't think you are above the other traders you are working with. Customers often find it mind-boggling that neighbouring stalls are friends rather than enemies as surely we're all competing for the same business. This just shows how little they see of the blood, sweat and tears that have got us there in the first place. Fellow traders are your friends, they will have seen whatever mess you've got yourself into before and be able to help you out of it. The kindness of other traders never ceases to astonish me; everyone forgets things, all equipment breaks, staff let you down. If you've been an arsehole all year, and have only spoken to people about how many portions you've sold (the worst kind of trader) no one is going to lend you a gas bottle, help you lift the fryer out of the car or give you a jump-start for your knackered van. You've got to have a chat. If you prefer to be alone then that's fine, but street food is a community and you've got to pitch in; if not you'll be out on your ear in no time.

'The biggest difference between running a restaurant and running a street-food business is when you see your fellow street-food traders you see a community rather than competition . . . it's so refreshing.'
Francesco, WANDERERS KNEADED

That's all before we even talk about customers. You'll have to explain your product approximately nine million times. People will ask you odd questions and use you as tourist information. People will ask if you have a chicken/gluten-free/vegan option. People will ask you reasonable things about who you are, whether your food affects their allergens and what your story is. And people will also tell you how to cook the food you've literally set up a business to cook; they'll lean into your stall and pick at food in a way that makes you think they've never been outside in their lives before. It's madness but you need to work out how you deal with all these interactions in an appropriate way. You've got to do it, so get on with it and be nice.

People are funny. We once did a really busy festival and we sold out of everything apart from chips. Unfortunately, because we were pretty new and complete morons, we didn't just have 'portion of chips' on the menu; at that point, they always came with other stuff. When we were in other places we had them on the menu for £3, so that's what we were selling them for. A lady came to the front, ordered some and asked the price, then said angrily, 'Well, you've just completely made that price up.' Well, yes, we have, alongside everything else in this business. The price had obviously been calculated at one point, but the underlying premise of this whole business, madam, is made up, the festival you are in is made up. You have moments like this where people will patronise, belittle and annoy you, but you just have to smile and wait for it to pass. And try not to roll your eyes so hard that you pass out.

Staff
At the beginning it'll probably just be you or you and whoever you set it up with. If you need anyone else for a one-off event, then you can bribe supportive friends. After that, if you're in a city, there are loads of agency businesses, which are a boon to

street-food businesses as they can help with ad hoc events and scheduling. They'll deal with all the legal requirements and taxes, and you can just book people when you need them. If you have regular spots, you're more likely to get the same person again and again, which makes your life easier as they (hopefully) don't need to be retrained each time. If you're out in the countryside, it can be more difficult, but this is where you really need to rely on your network of street-food traders; some share staff or they can pass on the numbers of those keen for temporary work. Facebook, community and WhatsApp groups can also be useful to find ad-hoc staff.

Once you get bigger and have a more permanent need for staff, then get some professional advice, give people a contract, holiday and decent pay, and offer them a sensible number of hours. You need to put them on payroll and organise their tax and NI contributions. Don't be a dick. Make sure you look after them. Street food incorporates a whole host of skills: you need to be a good chef, keep hygiene standards up, be able to talk to customers, deal with payments and with other staff, be capable of being outside and on your feet all day, and be able to cope with the manual labour of setting up and packing down. Good staff are worth their weight in gold, so don't take the piss, otherwise they'll get poached or just leave. You'll never realise how much easier they made your life until they're gone. Also, be wary of anyone who swans in telling you how great a chef they are. Often they get sick of doing just the one product (as is generally the only option in a street-food stall) and see certain parts of the job as beneath them. Best isn't always best; I prefer someone who turns up on time and isn't a twat.

'The biggest issue is someone's work ethic. I don't mind if you don't know how to do something if you're willing to learn. It blows my mind when people don't have any work ethic, but that's maybe just because we've all been working our asses off for so long.'

Lee and Sinead, BONG BONGS

As many street-food stalls specialise in one product you can train and mould anyone who is willing to learn to make that product. This may take more time, but it's better than someone consistently swanning in twenty minutes late to tell you how you could improve your business (after you've been running it for three years). Advice can help you see the light, but unsolicited advice for non-issues can be pretty wearing.

To motivate employees some businesses offer target-based bonuses, which, once hit, means that the employee then gets a percentage of the takings. This is great for motivation, especially if you're leaving them alone on the stall or it's going to be really busy and you need to keep them engaged throughout the day. Each business is different, though, and you have to figure out what works best for you.

As street food has traditionally been cash-based (though this looks set to change as a result of Covid-19), people do worry about stealing. There are measures you can put in place which all evolve out of you having a firm grasp on your business – for example, how much stock you sold should equal how much money you have. Work out a really basic calculation of how much you should make from the stock you have and keep an eye on it. Due to the introduction of card machines you can now put everything through an electronic system so it will clearly state how many portions you have sold and therefore how much money you should have. Don't rely solely on this, though, because if someone is going to steal, they will find a way. Always know how much money you're supposed to have with the stock available.

You are responsible for your company culture. There is a link between company culture and profitability; if you make it a nice, entertaining, rewarding place to work, your staff turnover will be lower, which means less stress for you and happier, harder-working staff who actually care whether you're a success or not. If you don't treat them well, then of course they'll feel under-appreciated, become lazy, and possibly see stealing from you as an option because they'll just be taking back what they feel is owed.

'Good staff are one of the most important elements of a successful business. Unfortunately, managing staff can sometimes feel like a revolving door; it seems to feel like as soon as you get a solid stable team, you lose your best member of the team, but it's never long before you have someone else trained up to take on their responsibilities. The sooner you accept that none of them will be with you

forever the better. I found this very stressful at the start, because I took it personally every time someone handed in their notice, or just couldn't be arsed to show up. I find staff respond better when there are clear structures in place, so they know exactly what you want from them. Also, make sure you nip any bad attitude or habits in the bud, otherwise you end up in a mess. Once they're trained up if you can encourage a fun, relaxed atmosphere while they still carry out their work to the best of their ability, then it comes across well to the customers and creates a good vibe. This has also helped me with recruitment, as staff are more likely to tell their friends how much they enjoy their jobs. When a few leave at once and you lose that momentum it's hard to get that back and you can see it in the sales ... Staff aren't going to know what to do if you don't know what to do, so you've got to know the job inside out so you can show them. And when you're not there you need to have a supervisor so that the rest of the guys have someone to look to. It's no good leaving a stall without someone in charge; staff always need someone to look to and if they don't have that it turns into carnage, and carnage equals loss in sales.'

Leo, Northfield Farm

You need to lead by example, know your stuff and be able to train your staff so they know it too. They're human, so have a chat and some fun. Communication is especially important to help with motivation and sales. Tell your staff what kind of day you're expecting so they can get into the right mindset for it. Different days demand different mindsets and different skills;

tell them what you need from them *that* day. Whether it's upselling to make as much money as possible, keeping an eye on stock levels, keeping an eye on change because you don't have much, pushing a certain product or doing a deep clean so that they don't get bored and waste time. Each day has different issues and the whole point of having staff there is to help you combat those problems, so tell them what they are and how they can help.

Invest in your staff, give them decent wages, training and real career progression – they are the ones that can take your business to the next level.

'I had a really good staff member who could run the business, but he didn't have a driving licence. So I paid for him to take a few lessons and take his test. It cost me £1,000, but it meant that if I wanted to have a weekend off I didn't have to close Broadway [Market], so it made financial sense really quickly. It changed my business overnight. And it meant I could literally give him the keys to the street-food business, and then I could focus on opening the café. It was a big risk as he could have just left us but he didn't, and even though they won't be there forever you can invest in their future and they'll appreciate it and hopefully stick around for longer.'

Carol, DEENEY'S

Every street-food trader has horror stories about crap staff they've had: people not turning up, people stealing, people being rude and people just being useless. Unfortunately, you are bound to encounter this from time to time, but generally these people are exceptions to the rule. If you do have a bad situation, mark it down as experience and move on. Don't let the bastards grind you down.

I had an experience where I'd booked an agency member who came to the stall and was completely astounded that we were even thinking of selling food on the street. He was early so I told him to go and have a coffee in the warm for a bit, and he replied, 'Well, I'm not sure I'll be coming back at all'. He did come back but then proceeded to slag off street food for the entire shift. It was a long and painful shift and everything I asked him to do seemed to be completely out-of-this-world unreasonable for him. At the end of his shift he helpfully told me, as if this had never occurred to me before in my life, 'Hey, you know what you need? A shop.' Thanks, mate. He then proceeded to tell me, 'This is all a lot of work, especially for a woman.' Luckily, at this point I could tell him to leave and somehow I managed not to punch him in the face. It sometimes feels like some people have been sent to test you. To add to it I was also four months pregnant. On the other hand, you have some absolute dreams; I once had a family emergency during a really busy shift. I told the agency guy what had happened and he just took over, got on with everything while I tried not to completely fall apart. So you win some, you lose some. Keep hold of the decent ones. Remember staff can bring expertise too:

'Looking back to the early years before we got properly organised, things were a lot harder; I wasn't naturally the most organised, list-driven person then. But the way we run things now is just so much easier and that's not just what I've learnt; everyone who has worked for Yum Bun has brought something. Particularly now, having someone who has come in from similar businesses and who brings their experience from those businesses has really helped the business move forward.'

Lisa, YUM BUN

Now on to the real nitty-gritty...

KEY POINTS

- If you have a business partner, ensure you have clear roles.

- Street food is a community.

- Staff thrive within clear structures.

- Learn from those around you (staff and other traders).

- A good company culture improves sales.

Chapter 7

What will you need?

Let's start at the very beginning

Before you apply to any markets or events, these are the absolute basics that you must do. Get ready to get your paperwork in order.

1. Create a name and a product and buy only the essential equipment needed to make said product (see equipment list below). Don't get excited and think you need all the lovely new shiny things – you don't. Buy the essentials and go from there.

2. Decide whether to register your company as a limited company, sole trader or partnership. Do some research and work out what's best. Sole trader and partnerships are easy to set up and have a pretty simple structure that requires relatively little paperwork compared to limited companies. They do, however, have unlimited liability, so if your company ends up in debt then all your personal assets are at risk. Setting up a limited company involves more paperwork, but they have their own legal identity, so your personal assets aren't as exposed. Do the research,

ask someone who knows more than you and talk it through. Whichever you choose, get it registered.

3. Get public and employee liability insurance. This covers you in case you make someone ill and they sue you. It is essential and nowhere will let you trade without it.

4. Register with the Nationwide Caterers Association (NCASS). Sometimes you come across organisations that are a godsend. NCASS is one of those; they are an absolute dream. They will talk you through everything. They will provide you with all the health and safety documents, advice and general knowhow that you need. You will get a big-ass folder containing all your documents so you can send them to prospective markets and look professional. You can also take all sorts of health and safety courses online so you actually know what you're doing.

5. Apply to your local council. You have to tell them you are setting up the business twenty-eight days before you sell anything so they can come and inspect your home. You need to have a Food Safety Management System (FSMS) in place and know about HACCP (Hazard Analysis of Critical Control Points), and be able to talk about it to your inspector and market managers. The whole point of FSMS and HACCP is to reduce the chances of food contamination and poisoning, so you don't make anyone ill and kill them (useful). You need to know this stuff and get to grips with it. Inspectors will come down harder on you if you sound like

you're just making it up or don't know the answers to simple questions, so make sure you know your stuff, sign up to NCASS and actually read and use your FSMS folder.

6. Everyone working on the stall needs, at a minimum, a Level 2 Hygiene Rating. As the owner of the business you need Level 3 and you should have HACCP and Fire Safety too. You can do all of this through NCASS.

7. Once you've been inspected by the council you will get a Food Hygiene Rating which people can look up online and that, by law, you have to display on your stall. Anything below 4 and you will have a very hard time getting onto any market or event. Sloppy hygiene kills people, so you need to be on top of this. Look around your home – is it clean? Do you have eight cats? Loads of housemates? You have to think about all these things if you're suddenly running a food business from your kitchen. Food inspectors have the right to inspect any food business within their opening hours, so you will get inspected on the street too. You need to take these seriously as the enforcement officer can close you down. They can also recommend prosecution, which can lead to a heavy fine, imprisonment or a ban on you ever managing a food business again. Fun stuff, eh?

8. Know your allergens and have an allergen table printed and kept visible on the stall at all points. Not knowing this stuff kills people, so it is not worth winging it, ever. You

need to have 'Ask about allergens' on the menu and be able to answer your customers' questions.

9. Get all your gas equipment checked by a gas engineer. Avoid domestic equipment where possible as it won't have the capacity or power you need. All gas equipment needs a flame failure device (thermocouple), which cuts off the gas and cuts out the flame so that you don't get gassed or blown up (which is helpful). Use your gas engineer, ask them for advice about using gas bottles and equipment. Gas canisters are, obviously, really dangerous but you often come across people with a strangely relaxed attitude towards them. Learn how to use them safely. I once saw (from afar) a guy detaching a gas bottle with a cigarette in his mouth and he'd not turned off the gas bottle. Safe to say, it did not end well and he went to hospital with multiple burns. It was horrendous. Learn how to use them so you can spot, hear or smell a dangerous connection 15 feet away. The same goes for fire extinguishers and blankets: ask your gas engineer for advice. Know what to do if something catches fire. When your business gets bigger you'll have to train your staff in this stuff, so you need to know how to use it.

10. Get all your electrical equipment PAT-tested (portable appliance testing). Even if you've just bought it, many markets and festivals will demand a PAT certificate no matter how old it is. It's also way more professional having a certificate rather than sending a collection of receipts to prove how old your lights are. You will need to know how

many amps you need for your set-up. You will be asked this all the time while applying for markets and festivals. Best to work it out when you have everything together and a PAT engineer available to ask for advice.

11. Get organised. There's a lot of paperwork involved in setting up a street-food business. Buy some folders. When you set up a business with HMRC you'll get approximately 10,000 letters from them; keep them in a folder. They all look the same, yet some have vital information on them which you'll need when doing tax returns. That time is stressful enough without trying to work out if you threw them out, hid them in your sock drawer or pinned them on the fridge. Once you've done your first tax return you'll know which numbers, letters and dates are vitally important. Write these down on the inside cover of the folder, this makes your future dealings with HMRC much less stressful. Easy.

'There's a tendency, if you don't feel comfortable with or know about something (like accounting) to just avoid it, but it's much better to get stuck in and learn how to do it. It's taken me ages to get to grips with all the aspects of the business, and it would have been so much easier and less stressful if I'd done that from the start, like with health and safety. It may seem really long and boring at the start, but once you get on with it you realise that it's not so bad. Get stuck into the details, it's all about the lists.'

Lisa, YUM BUN

Equipment

Buy the very best you can afford. Decent equipment will allow you to run things smoothly and make more money, so it is not the place to skimp. However, be sensible; don't bankrupt yourself at the start by buying a £1,000 fryer. Buy a decent one, or a second-hand one, and once you know how vital it is to your business, then invest in the best one possible. Slow and steady is the best way forward, otherwise you end up with stuff you don't need.

'We never had investment; we literally just bought a table and a pot with £50 for our first day, then made £300 and bought a gazebo with that. That's why I find it weird when people now turn up on day one with a £50,000 food truck. We started off doing pulled pork at farmers' markets and now we're doing mac and cheese at festivals. It's very different, so if I'd started off in a van made for pulled pork it wouldn't have worked, we wouldn't have been able to develop.'

Anna and Tony, ANNA MAE'S

Once you know what you need and are ready to invest, remember, 'buy cheap, buy twice'. This stuff needs to be hardwearing, it's going to be transported loose in the back of a van, lifted in and out and probably get dropped a few times, so it needs to be tough.

It took us ages to buy our first decent fryer because it cost £1,000. It took us a long time to save and then to actually part with the cash because we were worried it wouldn't be worth it.

It changed our output overnight. We were so much quicker; it was so much more powerful and the food was better because of it. It's scary spending that money, but if it's going to take your business to the next level you need to do it, you need to keep re-investing your profits back into your business. But before you spend the big bucks do two things:

1. Make sure it is essential to your business. How is it going to improve your business and make you more money?

2. Do some research, look at what other traders are using, ask them if it's any good. If you see the same grill on every stall, then that's a pretty good indicator that it's a quality grill.

Street-food traders do end up with quite a lot of kit, so ask around and see if anyone has some old stuff you can buy off them to get you started. Make sure you see the equipment in action before you hand over any cash though, and ensure that it has been PAT- or gas-tested recently.

If you buy new, check the warranty. Most places will have a customer service team to help you get to grips with it all. New equipment still needs to be PAT- or gas-tested before you start trading.

If you're buying an entire business from someone, make sure everything has been checked and works. Go and see it in action first. Pitches are generally not transferable, so if someone is selling you their pitch on a certain high-profile spot, then don't just take their word for it; check it's legit and get that confirmation yourself.

Carts, trucks and gazebos

What are you going to sell from? You may have been seduced by the old fire engines or the cute bike carts with their lovely parasols, or perhaps you want the space and freedom of a gazebo. They've all got their benefits.

Truck or trailer

Pros

- **Good looking:** If you've fitted it out well and have good branding, then you are instantly smart, cool and presentable, which is particularly good for private events.

- **Quick and easy:** You drive up to the event, open your hatch and you're ready to cook. There's no hour-long set-up wrestling with a gazebo.

- **Warm and dry:** You are protected from the weather. You're not going to blow away in a van (hopefully).

Cons

- **Size:** Once you have your equipment and stock in there can you actually do anything? At festivals a lot of vans are used as a glorified till while all the cooking happens in a gazebo out the back due to space constraints.

- **Height:** Can you stand up straight? Will you break your back? Are you able to chat to your customers?

- **Speed:** If you have an old vintage van, how long will it take you to drive anywhere? Are the extra hours worth it?

- **Age:** It may look cool, but is it reliable? Can you get spare parts for it? Will you be charged for taking it into town centres, for example the Ultra Low Emission Zone (ULEZ) charge.

- **Security:** Where will you park it? Theft is a worry but so is vandalism – graffiti across your new van is not a good look.

- **Qualifications:** Are you able to drive it? Will anyone else be able to?

'At our first event we had fridges in the back of the van which weren't strapped shut, so we got to the event and there was food all over the back of the van. I also didn't build the caravan right, so when it rains the water runs down the hatches and into the caravan. Just what you want.'

Alex, PINK PEPPERCORN

Don't buy your van before you understand your business thoroughly as you need to make sure it fits your needs.

'We were looking at buying second-hand but a lot of the vans had griddles and fryers in them, whereas we needed more of a kitchen, because we needed lots of worktop space so that we could fillet fish and deal with the crabs and lobsters, and we needed to have one side for raw and one side for cooked. So we had to buy new because we knew exactly what space we needed.'

Fenella and Kirsty, THE SEAFOOD SHACK

Gazebo

Pros

- **Cheap:** You can buy a terrible one for £60 (don't do this) or a fairly decent sturdy one for around £300.

- **Simple:** You don't need a qualification to use a gazebo.

- **Flexible:** You can change your whole set-up inside, the gazebo stays the same and you can set up anywhere.

Cons

- **Time and effort:** You have to physically set up and pack down your stall every day.

- **Weather:** You are more exposed to the elements. We once did a festival which was closed after one day due to extreme weather. While waiting to see if we could drive off site we saw a gazebo fly across a field with a man running desperately behind it. You wouldn't have that issue with a van.

'At the start we didn't know what we were doing so bought really stupid equipment. We bought a garden gazebo from Argos, we didn't have weights so used to tie it to the van, and when we did have weights we got the big plastic ones you fill with water, and our BBQ was from the sale in Homebase. We thought we were really cool.'

Lee and Sinead, BONG BONGS

Cart

Pros

- **Cost:** Cheaper than a truck but still smart and presentable, which is particularly good for private events.

- **Height:** Same level as customers, which is great for chat and eye contact.

- **Versatile:** You can set up in places trucks can't fit or aren't allowed, such as public squares, train stations, office courtyards. You'll need a pedlar's licence to have full freedom but as long as you can move it the world is your oyster!

Cons

- **Transportation:** How do you transport it? You can only cycle or push it so far.

- **Out in the open:** You are very exposed to the elements and to customers; you don't have walls or a table to hide behind.

- **Space:** Only good for low-prep items such as waffles or ice cream. There's not much space for volume either.

'We got a pedlar's licence, which is a really old law meaning you can travel from place to place and sell wares and food – as long as you can move, then you can sell from your cart. So a policeman came round to our house and signed us off. We were just doing snacks from a cart, but it's what got us started on the street.'

Manjit and Michael, MANJIT'S KITCHEN

Basic equipment set-up includes

- Cooking equipment, so whatever you need for your product, such as a grill, fryer, bain-marie, rice cooker, etc.

- Gas for cooking equipment, and a spanner for the connections.

- Extension lead for electric cooking equipment and lights. Buy a 12-amp adapter plug too, so that you don't get caught short at a market without the proper connections.

- Menu board and allergen sheet. Menu should be clear and have the allergen sheet stuck to the back of it for easy reference and access when needed.

- Signage.

- Market clips, G-clamps and cable ties to hold everything together. You can get these from your local hardware store.

- Fridge or cool box and ice packs. If you're doing this by yourself, don't get one so big that you can't lift it once it's full. Get two which you can move. This also helps keep the temperature regulated if you're not opening the same one constantly.

- Hand-wash facilities. There are excellent portable hand-wash basins from Teal. You need a sink, anti-bacterial soap and blue roll accessible at all points. Washing your hands is vital, remember Covid-19 guys ...

- Latex gloves and aprons. Make sure you understand what they're for (more on this below).

- First-aid kit, with burn cream.

- Fire blanket and extinguishers. Work out what you need for the equipment you have, buy the right blanket and extinguisher, and learn how to use them. Staff need to know how to use them too and in what situations, so you definitely need to know – there's no point in having them otherwise (see box for what you might need should the worst-case scenario occur).

- Health and safety document folder. Photocopy all your documents, put them in a folder and have them in your set-up box at all times so you can show them when inspected.

- Temperature record book, probe and probe wipes. Keep these handy as you should be using these things a lot. Know what information you need to record for your product and how often.

- A sneeze guard. This is a piece of plexiglass plastic that forms a barrier between the customer and the food. You can buy bent ones which will stand up on their own; however, these will often break and crack. For more longevity just get a thick sheet of plexiglass and use G-clamps to keep it upright.

- Antibacterial spray and blue roll. Antibac spray

needs to be 'fast acting', so with a spray-and-leave time of forty seconds or less. This is one of the questions the health and safety visitor will ask on their inspection, so make sure you know and actually abide by it.

- Cable-tie cutters. Just buy one pair. The number of times I've seen people slice their hands or arms open because they were trying to cut a cable tie with a knife. Don't be that person; just buy one and it'll save you time and injury.

- Storage boxes to keep all the miscellaneous stuff in. Have one for clips, tablecloths, sprays, etc, and a separate one for dry foodstuffs, such as seasonings. Perishable food goes in the fridge at all times.

- Lights. This is not necessary if you're just doing lunchtime events; however, they are essential for pretty much anything else. They'll make your spot stand out and look more attractive. Make it nice, be creative. Don't just buy floodlights, they will make you look like a building site. Think of how nice restaurant lighting is; have something like festoon lights at the front and, by all means, have a stronger one at the back so you can actually see what you're doing. Just don't forget about the overall 'look and vibe' of the stall.

Fires involving...

Oil or fat: Fire blankets and a 6-litre wet chemical extinguisher.

Waste bin fire: A 6-litre water fire extinguisher.

Electric fire or one involving a generator: A 2-litre CO_2 fire extinguisher.

Barbecue fire: A 6-litre water fire extinguisher. They all need to be maintained and serviced regularly.

Van, carts and trailers will have everything inside and attached, but if you're starting with a gazebo you will need:

- 3x3-metre gazebo with walls and weights. 3x3 metres is the standard size for any market or event. People do get 6x3 metres for festivals and the like; others get a smaller 2x2 metres if they feel they don't need the space. Best to start with a 3x3 as that is the expected and most common size, and work from there.

- Tables are essential, obviously, but it's also important for health and safety reasons that you don't store food on the floor. Think about if it rains, and the floor's wet, what will you do? Bear this in mind when plotting the layout of your stall. Where will you put everything? Get tables that are at the right height; they exist, so you don't have to break your back using low tables. Make life easier for yourself.

- Most places will insist on flooring. Make sure it's non-slip and thick enough so if you do have spillages it won't stain the floor beneath you. A good place to start is Halfords, where you can get jigsaw garage flooring which is light and pretty cheap.

- A stall skirt covers the legs of the table at the front of the stall. It makes the difference between looking like you're at a car-boot sale and at a street-food market. Be creative, you can make a huge difference to the overall look of the stall with small things like this.

Layout and queues

While organising your stall layout think about the flow of service. What do you need to do and in which order? Are you right-handed or left-handed? Every movement counts in a busy service so are you wasting them? Work out where staff will stand. Will you be on top of each other? Are all the key components in one corner of the stall? Organise it while you're still quiet so that when it does get busy you're not flapping around knocking into each other.

It's important to keep customers moving. Learning how to

manage your queue effectively is essential to get any return business. A queue can be stressful, but it can also be your greatest asset so know how to manage it to keep your customers happy. Don't just take everyone's order at once and make them wait for thirty minutes. Do it in phases. Your staff will be less stressed when faced with five orders rather than twenty and it means your queue is moving and that by the time your customer gets to order they know they haven't got long to wait. Make sure you have a system in place to ensure that people get what they actually order. Don't rely on customers remembering – they won't or they'll just lie and throw your whole system into the air by taking someone else's order. Use names, numbers or buzzers.

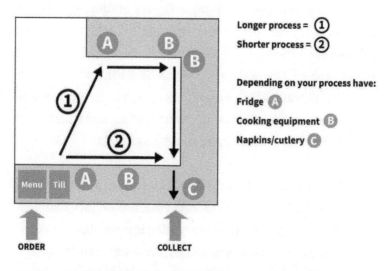

N.B. If you are able to have your grill/bain-marie etc. near the front, then do it. It's fantastic for creating drama, colour and delicious smells, and for giving people something to put on their social media. Deep-fat fryers, however, are an exception to this rule; they're not very exciting and they can have the tendency to make people feel unhealthy (I wonder why).

Health and safety

Health and safety is obviously really important; it ensures you don't kill anyone, and it makes your food better. It's also a legal requirement, so you have no choice in the matter. People sometimes seem to have the mad idea that because you're outside, health and safety becomes less important. It is *twice* as important, as you don't have the base level of a clean, sealed kitchen, so you need to be aware of everything that could be a contaminant. The floor, the weather and other traders are just the starting point. You need to be super-aware and know how to keep your stall a health and safety dream rather than nightmare.

To do this, and to have started a food business, you should have done your food hygiene training to Level 2 minimum and Level 3 if you're the owner. Do this through NCASS; they have a number of courses included in their membership. Having done this, you should know everything you need to about health and safety. Top-notch. Well done. I'm not going to go through it all again, but here are some points to remember, and which often seem to be forgotten on many street-food stalls:

- The purpose of gloves is that they are clean and hygienic. People seem to forget this and believe that once you have them on everything is magically clean. They carry on handling money, touching their face, eating food and even, sometimes, going to the loo with their gloves on. The only thing they are keeping clean at this point are their hands. Not the point.

From the very beginning you need to work out a system that separates food and money handling. Money is unbelievably dirty; we just don't think about it as we handle it every day, but faecal matter is found on 14 per cent of bank notes and 10 per cent of bank cards. There's a brand called Easy Glove which is worth checking out as a solution. As a basic rule don't leave the stall with your gloves on; they are completely pointless once you leave the stall and just make you look like you have no idea about health and safety, or that you have a strange latex fetish. They are thin and disposable purely for hygiene reasons, so change them regularly. If you look at them and wouldn't put them in your mouth, they shouldn't be touching food. *NB: Don't ever actually put your gloves in your mouth.

- Get a sink and some antibacterial soap and use it. SIMPLE.

- Know what temperatures your food has to be stored at, check the temperature and record it. Then you won't kill anyone, and everyone will have safe, deliciously cooked food. EASY.

- Wear aprons in the stall, not outside it. Don't wear one to the loo or the wholesaler as, like gloves, this defeats the point of the apron. It's a clean barrier from your dirty outside clothes to the food and also the food to your clothes. If you're outside your stall in an apron, you've missed the point.

- If you have food laid out in front of the customer, you'll need a sneeze guard so that people don't sneeze or accidentally spit on or poke the food. It'll amaze you how often people will try to reach in and grab something, thinking it's TOTALLY FINE. This is especially prevalent when people have had a bit to drink. Or when they're just terrible human beings.

- Street food involves a lot of lifting, so don't break your back. Bend from your knees and check if something is too heavy by trying to move it with your foot in the first instance. If you can't move it with your foot, grab a mate. Don't try to be a hero, just ask for help. Really, no one is impressed by how much you can lift.

- Make sure you have what you need in a first-aid kit for burns, cuts, etc. Accidents do happen, but they happen less often when people get adequate training. Fryers are full of hot oil, knives are sharp, gas bottles are heavy; make sure people know how to use the equipment at hand. You might as well live.

- Have the appropriate tools for the job. Don't cut cable ties with a knife, don't light a grill with a blowtorch, buy a trolley to ease the lifting. Don't make things harder for yourself.

Once you have become more aware of health and safety you will see shocking instances of people behaving like idiots around food. People handling raw meat and then passing the finished burger to you with the same glove. People keeping pots of raw prawns out on the table in the sun with no refrigeration at all. People rubbing their face with their gloved hand and then dealing with your food. People tasting what they've made and then double dipping the spoon. A lot of it is people just behaving like they would in their home kitchen, which is fine if you're the only one eating those germs, but you can't sell people that stuff. They expect more from you as they are *literally* paying you. A lot of these actions are instinctive reactions from cooking at home, so you have to be vigilant and make a conscious effort to think about not doing them at all times. It will become second nature to you. If you're surrounded by traders who seem to have never learned anything about health and safety, don't let the bastards drag you down. Be diligent, focus on your own stuff and don't buy food from them. Be smug in the knowledge that you're at the top of your game.

KEY POINTS

- Be organised.

- Know how to use your equipment safely.

- Work out what you really need and invest when you can.

- Remember your health and safety training – you did it for a reason.

Chapter 8

What will it cost?

The very nature of street food is that most of the time you are in different places with different audiences. This means that the fixed variables that restaurants rely on are thrown out of the window. Rent, stock, staffing and power can vary massively at every event. You need to be aware of this, work out how to manage it and be able to spot a dodgy deal from a mile off.

I'm way more sceptical now, especially with events that seem too good to be true or have large pitch fees. I'd rather look for a percentage of sales than a set pitch fee, so if it's terrible weather you only lose a percentage. I wouldn't go for an event now which is attended by ten thousand people with a pitch fee of £700 plus VAT, plus electricity.'

Francesco, WANDERERS KNEADED

'I look at the rent: if it's more than 10 per cent of what I expect to take, then it's not worth it. Also, demographic; we don't appeal to a lot of people, we know that the mainstream events don't work for us. We have to have an audience up for an interesting experience.'

Carol, DEENEY'S

Rent

This can vary massively. For markets it can be anything from £15 to £200 a day. For festivals and events, you may be charged per square foot, or a percentage of your takings. As there's such a range you need to take each one as it comes and analyse whether it's worth it. The basic things to think about are:

a) Is the rent reasonable for what and where it is?

b) How much actual trading time do you realistically have?

c) Is it possible to make a profit?

When we first started we paid £15 a day. This is amazing for a new business as it gives you the freedom to basically give anything a go and mess up without too much worry. I'd advise everyone to start off on a cheap market and see if it works before you bother trying for the more expensive ones. Often they need you to have traded elsewhere before they take you on anyway.

Council-led markets are often the cheapest markets. We work from a council market for which we pay £25 to the council but then pay a further £30 to the market association who manage the day-to-day running and setting-up of the stalls. Lunchtime markets near offices can vary from £15 to upwards of £180 and this is generally for, at the most, three hours' trading. The average in London is around £110, so you really need to work out if you can shift enough portions quickly enough to make a profit.

Many markets and events have worked out that in some instances street-food traders are making way more than them, so have in turn decided to take a piece of the pie. This comes in several guises: rent plus a percentage of your takings; rent plus a percentage of your takings with a cap; or others who just take a percentage of your takings or a base-rate rent, whichever is the higher amount. The percentages can vary massively from 10 to 35 per cent. When the percentage is high you need to work out whether it's worth it or not. Don't get seduced by the nice emails and the fancy event page, but instead consider whether you are going to be able to make a profit? On the other hand, if it's just a percentage of your takings and there's no other rent fee payable, then it can be a safer bet because the event organisers are clearly invested in you doing well; whereas if it's just a fixed fee you need to know what you're getting for that and why it is fixed: what are they basing it on?

Then we get on to festivals. These vary hugely and you get what you pay for. Take Glastonbury: you're paying around £6,000 to be in a prime spot. That's basically for a week. You then factor in how much stock you need to buy to make that money back; how many staff you'll need to pay to sell it; all the power, travel, etc, and you can see already that it's a pretty big gamble. On the other hand, you're in front of the main stage at Glastonbury, so you've got a decent chance of selling shedloads.

Glastonbury is obviously the granddaddy of festivals, but there are plenty of other smaller, nicer and less terrifying festivals to choose from. I'd highly recommend doing a smaller one before killing yourself on a huge one. Work your way up and get a feel for how well you operate on a larger scale. Rents are slightly lower at smaller festivals and they might be better suited to your product. Festivals are also run and organised in sections, so there may be the main section where the traders are chosen and organised by a big festival subcontractor and then there are other (often smaller) sections which are run by the festival itself. These can be specialist and often cheaper, though obviously these are quite rare. It's worth doing the research. Ask others who have traded there, and ask people who have actually been to the festival about where they ate.

The fact is that wherever you go rents can vary massively. It sometimes seems like the organisers – especially at smaller markets where there are fewer factors at play – are just blindly making it up rather than working out what's fair. In the last week alone, I have been sent various emails for events where in one instance the rent was £300 + VAT + 20 per cent of total takings per day, which is, quite frankly, daylight robbery. Especially as there's a very successful market just around the corner that charges £100 a day. Another email for a sporting event I received through the council quoted me £300 + VAT for three days' trading, which is a reasonable price; however, they are hiring out gazebos for the weekend for £250. Considering that a standard gazebo costs about £200 new, this is taking the piss and seems to be an effort to prey on people who don't have much experience.

Be wary of what people are charging you and see if it compares to similar events nearby. This is one of the massive pitfalls when you first start: you get drawn into these fancy-sounding events and then they rob you blind. Do the calculations on the rent and work out how many portions you need to sell to cover it. Are you able to do it, in the time available, to break even? Just because something is expensive and they've sent you a fancy press package does not mean that the streets will be paved with gold. If the event has been running for a few years, ask them how many visitors they have had? How did the other traders do? You can also ask who the other traders were and then contact them to find out the truth. If the event organisers have nothing to hide, then this should all be pretty easy to find out.

This is where the community of traders is so important: we can all protect each other from being burned by the same bad experiences. The organisers often believe that they hold all the power, that we all depend on them to make a living. However, due to the boom in street food and the plethora of events, markets, festivals and food halls there are now more and more options for us to make money. So, if someone is systematically screwing over trader after trader, we can spread the word, take a stand, and in the end they'll be the ones without an event.

These things do still take trial and error as events can take you by surprise. It will take you a while to work out who wants your food and where they are. Do market research on the six Ps:

1. **P**eople: Who are the other traders? Who are the customers? Is this your target audience? Does it fit with your brand?

2. **P**itch fees: Is it reasonable? What do you get for it?

3. **P**lacement: Where are you going to be at the event? In a dingy corner by the toilets or next to the main stage?

4. **P**roducts: What are people selling? Is there actually a market for what you're selling? Are the products sold there something you'd be happy to be associated with? Would you eat there?

5. **P**rices: What are people selling and how much for? What are customers willing to spend?

6. **P**ortions: Do people want full meals or stuff to share? What time of day is the busiest? What are people doing there? How much would you want to eat at that event?

'We work out which events to do through experience, by asking other traders, going on the website and looking to see if their customers are the type of people who would buy our food, by knowing our audience and asking friends and traders who have been to the event. We ask loads of questions too. Where are we going to be located? How many tickets? How many other traders? It's still a gamble though. At the start we had a two-to-one hit rate; now it's bit better. But even a job that was good last year can be a dud job this year because of the weather or because they've put more traders in. It's all

*cyclical. You've got to stick it out and hold your nerve to
see the overall picture.'*

Anna and Tony, ANNA MAE'S

Stock

Before starting at a market people are often worried about how
many portions to bring. Best practice is:

a) Go to the market the week before, sit there, see how busy
it is and get a feel for the place.

b) Work out how much you need to sell to make a profit. In
other words, work out your break-even analysis. More on
this later.

c) If it runs for a few days rather than just one, take two
days of stock with you on the first day. Then you have
enough if it's super-busy (and you can get more that
night) and if not, you can use it for the next day.

d) Ask other traders on the market for an average number
of portions. However, this can be misleading for a variety
of reasons. Regular traders will have regular customers,
so they will always be busier than first-timers. Your
products may be wildly different and so will appeal to
different people. They may not tell you, or they may over-
exaggerate or under-exaggerate. So don't take it as
gospel.

'After messing up quite a few times, we started asking ourselves, 'What would we be happy with?' Because we kept getting it wrong, bringing so much stock and then being disappointed. So we'd work out our costings and then say, 'What would we be happy to walk home with?' We'd forget about all the stories we'd heard from other traders that so-and-so made five grand there; we were just never near that so, as soon as we started saying what we'd be happy with, rather than aiming for an imaginary figure, then we started to be all right and not so disappointed. You're then not at a massive loss, and you've not got a load of stock left over. You're okay with what you've made.'

Lee and Sinead, BONG BONGS

Even after working out how much stock you need, at the start you will learn by trial and error. Different events and markets will experience different levels of footfall. Even at the same market footfall can vary dramatically week by week due to:

a) Weather.

b) Events nearby.

c) Big national events (sports matches or public holidays).

d) Public incidents, terrorism, pandemics, marches, etc.

It's worth keeping an eye out for any of the above when prepping how much stock you're going to take. Sometimes, even when all the odds appear to be in your favour (think sunny weather, a special event nearby), it can be completely dead for no reason at all. It's an anomaly when this happens, but it does happen. I worked in a big restaurant in central London during the 2012 Olympics. The whole world was coming to London, so we prepared ourselves. We employed extra staff, spruced the place up and placed big orders. It was our quietest summer ever; the tubes, restaurants and streets were deserted. Locals fled the city, regular tourists didn't come and those that were here were just focused on the Olympics and didn't bother with anything else.

Once you've been running for a while, you'll get to know what factors can lead to you having a decent day. They may well be different factors to those of the stall next to you. When you have a good day or a bad one, write down which factors were at play so you can start to see a pattern.

Staff
Different markets run for different times. Therefore, lengths of shifts are different. You may be doing a lunchtime market and can set up by yourself but need someone for the lunch rush and pack down, which will be for between three and four hours. Other times you'll do a market that is open all day with both the lunch and dinner rush, so you end up needing someone for ten hours a day. Unless you're doing the same market or event week in week out, these hours will vary, which makes it another thing to keep an eye on. It also makes it difficult to hold on to decent staff if you don't have regular shifts.

Power

Some places will provide electricity as part of the rent; other places will charge you seemingly random amounts for electricity. Know how many amps your set-up needs, work this out when you buy your equipment and get it all PAT-tested. Don't wing it and guess; you'll end up with too little, and it'll constantly cut out and screw over your (and others') trade.

Gas is the most reliable power source. It's more powerful than electricity, and with it you're truly independent. If all your equipment is gas-powered, then you can set up pretty much anywhere and won't be affected when other traders blow the electric supply. That being said, you can't use gas indoors, so if you're planning on doing a lot of indoor events, you'll need a full electric set-up too. Once you've got your gas set-up, speak to your gas engineer about the right size of canister to use for the equipment you have. Particular fryers are only any good if they have two 19kg canisters or above to be able to get the full power they need to do their jobs. Grills and hobs can use smaller 13kg ones. Speak to your gas engineer as they can advise you on this stuff. Use the right ones and service will be a whole lot quicker and smoother.

Once you've been doing this for a few weeks you'll get a better idea of how much gas you use per service and work out your costings from there. Gas bottles are a nightmare as it's quite hard to judge how much is left in one and people often work it out by just lifting them. How heavy they feel is therefore completely dependent on how tired you are. But you will get better at estimating and, if in doubt, have a spare. Don't feel like a failure if you run out – it happens to the best of us. Just ask around, someone may be able to help you out or know where you can get one close by.

Location

Location, location, location. With some festivals and markets you have to slog it out in a dingy corner somewhere and only slowly move up to the better spots once there's space. This sometimes means forking out for a bit of a shit spot just to get your foot in the door for the months or years to come. This is playing the long game, where there seem to be very few rules and zero promise that it will work out in the end. Sometimes it comes down to how reliable you are, sometimes it's about who the manager's mates are. Very rarely is it actually to do with the food. Sure, you can't have similar products next to one other, but the politics of positions are a murky area. However, people do leave and people do move up, so don't be polite and wait to be asked; express your interest. Often the empty spots won't get offered to whomever is next in line, but given to who asked first.

'I've learnt that you have to be more bolshy than you may naturally be. For example, if we've been put in a shit spot we've learnt not to just go along with it, I'm now able to say, "No, we've come a long way and we deserve that good spot as much as anyone else. What can you do to make this fairer?"'

Beth and Jim, SEADOG

Contracts

Across the majority of markets people don't have contracts – some do but most don't – so once you've got yourself up and running, don't just stay on the same market. It's good that you're dedicated to them, but you need to cover your back, because even if you've been turning up week after week for five years, don't think that you're safe for life. Things change, land changes hands and, especially in city centres, people want to repurpose it and build more flats for oligarchs. So cover your back, do a range of markets so if something does happen to one of them you still have options available to you. Don't be in the position that you've only ever traded in one place; try other stuff out, get some other contacts. Who knows what you might find?

If you do manage to land yourself a contract, well done! Hopefully this means you can run your business more efficiently as the variables will have been cut down significantly. Read the contract carefully, make sure you don't sign away your business and be aware of the small print. Some markets will give you yearly contracts, others are just weekly rolling contracts. Both have their benefits.

Bear in mind

It is really hard to find a decent trading spot which is open seven days a week. They are few and far between, and if they're any good they'll have a long waiting list. You'll work out after a while which markets and events are worth your time, but may only end up being two or three days a week, so you need to work out if you can make enough in those few days to tide you over for the whole week. This is especially true if you're doing the festival circuit: you spend the whole summer in various fields but you have nothing booked in for the rest of the year. Is it feasible as a yearly income? What do you need to budget for? This is basic business advice, but if you've had a good week or summer, don't go mad and splash the cash. Cashflow issues are one of the biggest reasons why businesses fail early on. Winter is coming. You might do a series of terrible events or need to repair your van. Save the money for a rainy day; you'll need it.

The maths part

No matter how much I bang on about how lovely and authentic your product needs to be you ultimately need to make money otherwise you won't survive as a business. How much do the ingredients cost? How much time does it take to make your product? How many people do you need? You need to work all this out and ensure you're actually making a profit from your product, otherwise you won't be going anywhere.

You need to know two basic things for your business to work:

1. The difference between gross and net profit margin

2. Break-even analysis

'One mistake I did make was not focusing on my numbers enough. I became too obsessed with the food and if your gross profit isn't on point, then your business isn't a business, it's a hobby.'

Dave, TACO DAVE

Gross and net profit margin

You need a way to work out if a market or event is worth doing, otherwise you're just doing every event blind, so you need to completely break it down to make it as simple as possible. Start with the raw material of your product. Let's say that costs you £1.40. You need your gross profit margin on that product to be 80 per cent so you can pay your bills. So you sell it for £7 because that gives you an 80 per cent gross profit margin (the other 20 per cent is the £1.40). Then, say you sell one hundred units, your total takings will be £700 but your *gross profit margin* will be £560, because that's what you have after the cost of your raw materials has been taken away. But to have made that money you will have also needed to change the raw product into a finished product, and to do that you need to pay for staff, gas and/or electricity, equipment, packaging and a place to sell it from. All of these things cost money. Your net profit is what is left after you've paid for those things, that's the money you've actually made. Gross profit is the money you have to pay for those essential things, and net profit is the money you've got after you've paid all your bills.

Break-even analysis

This is the most basic calculation you need. When you get sent a rent bill, sit down with the numbers and do this calculation. Here you go, some lovely maths:

- Sale price of product = a

- Cost of product = b

- Unit profit = a – b

To work out how many portions you need to sell to cover the rent you do the following calculation:

$$\frac{\text{Rent}}{\text{Unit profit}} = \text{Number of portions you need to cover the rent}$$

That's the base of the equation. You can then add extra stuff to this, depending on what your circumstances are. An obvious one to add is staff costs. So:

$$\frac{\text{Rent} + \text{Staff costs}}{\text{Unit profit}} = \text{Number of portions you need to cover the rent}$$

So, for example, if you did an event and the rent was £100, your cost of product was £1.40 and the sales price of your product was £7. You've also got two staff working for 8 hours at £10.55 an hour, so you would need to sell 48 portions (or make £336) to break even.

$$\frac{\text{Rent} + \text{Staff costs}}{\text{Unit profit}} = \text{Number of portions you need to cover the rent}$$

$$\frac{£100 + (16 \times £10.55)}{(£7 - £1.40)} = 48 \text{ portions}$$

$$\frac{£268.80}{£5.60} = 48$$

You can keep adding costs to the top of the equation, such as fuel, travel, etc, and you'll work out how many portions you need to cover your costs. This is what's known as your break-even analysis. BINGO.

Please note: I've done this in portions rather than pounds so it's clear to you on the day whether you're close to breaking even without having to count your cash-drawer every 10 minutes. If you prefer to work it out in cash, then you just multiply the number of portions you need by your sale price.

You need to know these numbers before you do any market or event because then you know how much you need to take and whether it is physically possible to do it in the time allotted. Once you know them you are in a much better position to negotiate pitch fees and spot a ridiculous fee from afar.

'For the business to be a success, everything has to be stripped back down and done properly . . . I wish we'd done it properly from the beginning. Yes, it's important to get up and serve customers the best food you can and make sure your gazebo is clean, but none of that really matters if you don't have the foundations in place: being on top of your accounts, your stock, your social media, and doing your profit and loss statements properly. It then makes it easier for you to work out where you can afford to put money in, and what you need to save.'
Lee and Sinead, BONG BONGS

Don't lose sight of the food

All this chat about numbers and you've forgotten what you came here for: a chance to be independent and feed people your food. The numbers are important, and to be a success you need to keep an eye on them, but don't lose sight of your food.

Being on the street gives you more flexibility compared to restaurants. You don't pay business rates for a start, so you can get more bang for your buck. You don't have fifty staff on the payroll or as many utility bills, so if you're savvy you can offer high-quality food for a reasonable price. This is part of the reason why street food is so exciting. People get to try things that were only previously available in very expensive restaurants.

'There have been some times where, due to demand, we have had to revert to buying things in. If, where possible, you can make it yourself, then you're not only cutting your costs, but you're improving your own credibility by having the knowledge behind you that says, quite comfortably, I made this and this is a great-quality product.'

Ranie, JAH JYOT

Passion is what divides the wheat from the chaff in street food, and customers can tell from a mile off if you don't care about your product. Let your passion shine through your business. It's your baby; you've got to love it, nurture it and be proud of it. Imagine being at a party and someone asks you why you set up your stall and your answer is, 'I did the calculations and I worked out that [insert product here] was the simplest way to make money'. Dear Lord, *no one* wants to talk to that guy. You want to talk to the person who is passionate about their food. They have a story they want to tell you and have a slightly mad glint in their eye while recommending a chilli. Do it for the passion, the adventure and the story, not for the slightly bigger profit margins.

'Focus on the ingredients: at the start when you're not making money you might think, "Wouldn't it be easier if I bought a cheaper this or that," but it ends up being a false economy. It's a learning curve, you've got to push on, but don't sacrifice the quality of your ingredients.'
Alex, PINK PEPPERCORN

If you are using the best ingredients, then tell your customers. Have it on a sign, in your name, tell the whole damn world. In recent years people are so much more aware of what they're eating and where it's coming from, and it's only going to get more important, so if you've got great suppliers shout about it. You may need to tweak your original product so that it makes financial sense and that's fine, it's all part of the learning process, but make sure that the tweaks still leave you with a quality product. There are certain products that are fantastic in your kitchen but no good on the street. They might take too long to make, go off too quickly, are difficult to source, are too much of a general faff or are just too expensive. Our initial idea was to do New England crab rolls. To find enough crab to do the experimental recipe was hard enough and I ordered 500g of crab online for £50 (did I mention we didn't know what we were doing?). It was delicious, but not a sensible way to set up a food business. To keep the quality (and enough crab in the roll) each roll would have cost £20. Or I would have had to mix in and spread it out with potato to make it go further. Then it's just a mediocre potato sandwich with a hint of crab and who wants that? So it was back to the drawing board.

Look at what is around you and accessible. Your first idea might not make business sense, but keep exploring it and work out how it can. Take a look and see what is popular or lacking in your area. What are you good at? What are you passionate about? All the social media marketing you need to do will be made so much easier if you care about your product and are proud of it. Great things can be created in adversity. Is there loads of waste after making your product? What, if anything, can you do with that? Try to make it as streamlined a process as possible. If you have lots of waste, that's money down the drain, so try to eliminate it.

'You've got to love what you're doing and have a product that you're really proud of. A lot of street food is selling it, and if you're not happy with, or proud of, your product then it can be pretty clear quite early on.'
Carol, DEENEY'S

Pricing

Do the maths and be sensible. Do not compare yourself to fast-food chains or sandwich shops because you are not the same.

You are a much smaller operation and are hopefully offering something much better. Farmers' markets are an excellent example of this. Yes, you can get your veg cheaper in the supermarkets but people choose to buy it from the farmers' market because they are buying into a lifestyle. They believe it's better because it's more traceable and more ethical. The attraction should be the same with street food; this is why when you have the best ingredients and suppliers you should shout about it!

As you can tell from this advice I am obviously not a financial advisor. Accountants must be screaming at this page. I am principally creative. I set up Shrimpy as a creative output and a space where we could be independent. The main reason was not to make a quick buck – there are far easier ways to do that. If that's your aim then fine, good for you, sell churros. If you are setting up the business for other reasons – creativity, love of food, fun, a desire to be outside all day, or for the sheer love of gazebos, then you need to create a product that you are proud of, which is tasty and at a price point which is fair for you both and the customer.

'Don't do it for the money because you can see the traders who do it for the money. You can make money, but you're not going to do it if that's your primary goal. You'll lose the quality and authenticity and, really, there're much easier ways to make money if that's what you want.'

Anna and Tony, ANNA MAE'S

Street food is all about stories. It often feels like a parody sketch when you read about someone romanticising the hell out of a cheese toastie, but it's what people want to hear and it gets people to your stall. Let your passion shine through; your story is what makes you different to the . . . other traders.

COSTS KEY POINTS

- No fixed costs.

- Look out for the 6 Ps.

- Work out your gross profit margin.

- Do a break-even analysis.

- No fixed costs = Higher-quality product.

Chapter 9

How will you manage the money?

God, accounts are boring. I can barely bring myself to write about them, but they are important, so here we go.

When running a small business, you have to wear a variety of hats: chef, accountant and a fez on your birthday. Some you'll find easier to wear than others (I'm looking at you, fez), but there's no point in avoiding the ones you hate because they'll catch up with you soon enough. Get on and get organised.

Get organised

As always, organisation is key. Get a box, a file or a folder to store your receipts in. Don't just leave them in a pile in the corner of your house or you will lose them and it'll just be annoying. Everything you buy, put the receipts in there. If you buy things online and get a receipt via email, save them in a special folder in your emails, or if you have a printer print them off and put them in the box.

Have a book or spreadsheet that you update after every trading day. Write down date, location and any other information you think may have affected trading, such as weather, a dodgy spot, equipment failure, whatever. This is *so* important because with this you can work out if you're improving or not, and with that, work out a reason why. You can then compare to last week, month or year, so it becomes easier to predict. Less stock wastage means more profit. Knowledge is power.

Now, you can set up a complicated spreadsheet and work out your taxes yourself, but for anyone who values their time and sanity I wouldn't advise this. Unless you studied maths to a high level or are an actual accountant it will drive you round the bend. There is so much accounting software out there to make your life so much easier. Especially now HMRC has made all tax digital, the softwares just link up, making your tax returns super-simple. Some of them even have apps so that you can upload your receipts on the go, meaning you never get left with a pile of receipts that you have to go through three days before your return is due. The software works out for you how much you owe and gives you advice on accounting issues. They give you fancy graphs and an overview of your business, so that you can easily see if you're running at a profit or a loss. They'll break down what you're spending, so you can see if you're spending too much on motor expenses or stationery. They'll tell you useful things clearly, including what your turnover is, when your return is due and how much that will be. Obviously, this will cost you a monthly fee, but they're typically cheaper than an accountant and can help you get to grips with the numbers side of things from the very start. You can start to analyse different aspects of your business and work out how you can run more efficiently.

I would encourage you to do your accounts, if you are able to, for at least the first year, so that you have a decent idea about your numbers and have a vague idea about how they work. This is your business, so you need to know what your turnover is and where you're spending the most money. Doing your own accounts for a while will give you a grasp of the figures and some knowledge, which you can then use to ask your accountant the right questions. Once you start asking accountants the right questions, that's when they can help you run a more efficient business and give you advice. Otherwise, they'll generally just get on and do the standard service. Know more, ask them questions and get more accountant for your buck. However, if you see that you're about to go over (or anywhere near) the VAT threshold, definitely get an accountant. If you are drowning under the accounting software and not filing your returns on time, get an accountant. They are worth the money as they often save you more than you pay them, especially if you turn out to be no good at organising your accounts and your business suffers as a result. If you are spending the majority of your time doing accounts, then you need help: your primary focus should be on the food and moving the business forward. If your focus is on receipts and desperately trying to interpret a confusing spreadsheet, *get an accountant.*

'I would definitely say do the accounts for a little bit just so you know how it works and then when you get sent the accountant bill you can remember how horrible it was doing it yourself. The last thing you want to do after

a week of selling food is to sit down with a whole load of
numbers. I didn't really know what I was doing.'
Anna and Tony, ANNA MAE'S

Doing your accounts is never going to be at the top of your to-do list. It will not fill you with joy. If it did you would be an accountant. However, this does not mean you can ignore it until the very last minute before a deadline. This is not good for your mental health and you won't remember what half the transactions were for. You'll be confused by vague receipts and a scrap of paper that just says, '£10 to Dave'. Who the hell is Dave? Instead, just set aside a little bit of time each week or each month to do the accounts for that period. That way it won't be quite so overwhelming, you'll be dead organised and you'll have a better handle on the business. You'll know where you spent too much and what you can do to help for the months ahead. Little and often is the name of the game.

Keep in mind what you have to pay

As ABBA put it, 'I work all night I work all day to pay the bills I have to pay', but what actually *are* those bills? You may see street-food businesses taking loads of money over the counter and think it's the quick way to get rich; it isn't. You can make some decent money if you're savvy, have a good product, get on some good pitches and have a bit of luck. Here's a lovely list of things you will have to pay for:

- Equipment.

- Stock.

- Wages.

- Health and safety training.

- Rent.

- Insurance.

- Road tax (if you have a vehicle, which you probably have).

- Value added tax (VAT). This is not an issue when you first start your business, but it is something to keep an eye on. Once your turnover for twelve months is over the VAT registration threshold of £85,000, you must pay a tax of 20 per cent of your takings. Bear in mind that VAT is on hot food, whereas cold food is exempt; VAT depends on your product and how you sell it. Get advice from an accountant and, if you do need to be VAT-registered, then get an accountant to deal with it all.

- Income tax, which is all dependent on how much you earn.

- National insurance contributions: a percentage of your and your employees' earnings.

- Corporation tax.

So don't run off into the sunset and splash your cash on a fancy new car if you've had a good summer. Pay all this and then see where you are; keep it all in mind. And on top of that you have to *literally* save for a rainy day. Weather is a shitter.

Financial help

When you first start up, have some savings put aside. Depending on what you're selling you can set up for as little as £1,000. Don't spend an obscene amount on equipment before you start. Start small, buy what you need to trade that first day and go from there. You can update and add more equipment when the time comes, but don't get sucked into a catering equipment website and believe that you need to buy the whole shop. Our first set-up cost us approximately £200. It consisted of a teppanyaki plate from Amazon, a tablecloth, some bowls and two aprons. It was as crap as it sounds, and I'd advise anyone against doing what we did, but it does show that it is possible. Needless to say, we very quickly worked out what we needed and bought it when we could afford it.

Don't quit your job just yet. Let's see how things go before you take that leap. Most decent markets and events are on the weekend so, for a while at least, you can work at your real job Monday to Friday and then do street food on the weekend. This way you get to give it a go without too much pressure about being able to pay your bills. You can then take holidays for the extra days in the week if you get a mid-week spot or event, or even go part-time. It sounds like hard work, but it'll give you a security net at the start. Loads of successful street-food traders started this way, and it's the only way unless you manage to land a seven-day market straightaway. Even that isn't a sure-fire way to ensure that you can pay your bills. When we started, we quit our jobs, had a five-day-a-week spot on a market (we had to work up to the weekend spots) and ran out of money pretty quickly, meaning both of us had to get part-time jobs. We finally got the weekend spot so were trading every day of the week, but it still took us around six months to then leave those part-time jobs and do street food full time. It was mental. We worked constantly and still felt like we were just scraping by. But we did it, and pretty quickly learned how to run the business in a more cost-effective way. Resilience and hard work are key.

'That first summer I was working at my job four days, having Fridays off so I could make the ice cream and then do Broadway Market on Saturdays. It went well and then I had the realisation, "Well, if I can do this, what else could I do?"'

Sophia, NONNA'S GELATO

Once you've found your feet there are all kinds of funding options available. The standard options are personal savings, borrowing from friends, family or the bank, but there are also plenty of other options out there which aren't your bank and can offer more than just money. A few examples of alternatives include:

- **The Prince's Trust:** If you're aged between

eighteen and thirty, The Prince's Trust can help to turn your big ideas into a business reality through their Enterprise programme. From training and mentoring to funding and resources, they provide help and support to really set your business off on the right foot.

- **Start-up loans:** A government-backed scheme designed to help people set up new businesses. They provide low-interest loans and access to free mentors from a pool of experienced advisors.

- **Funding Circle:** A peer-to-peer lending marketplace that provides funds for credit-worthy businesses at decent rates and with no early repayment fees.

- **Liberis:** A lending scheme funded by the government. You only pay back a percentage of what you take monthly, meaning that you're not stuck with a fixed fee through the quieter periods.

- **iZettle Advance:** Similar to Liberis, iZettle offers cash advances against future sales. Depending on your takings, you can get loans of different sizes and they just take a percentage of your card takings each month, so you don't have to even think about putting the money aside to pay it back.

- **Crowdfunding:** Make a good sell, promise lovely perks, shares or freebies to your investors, and get the money. Whether you choose an investment, loan, donation or reward-based set-up determines what the investors expect in return.

'We both put some money we had borrowed from our families into the business. And because we were mainly using seafood there was quite a lot of European funding at the time for projects that were involved in street food and the promotion of the seafood industry in north Devon, so we actually got a bit of money from them, which paid for our equipment.'

Beth and Jim, SEADOG

'I worked with the Prince's Trust: I'd applied in the summer and did a three-day course, and because I'd done those few days I had more pieces to the puzzle and so could answer more of the business-plan questions more clearly. So I finished my business plan – it is one of the most valuable tools a business can have. It blows my mind that some people don't have one. You could have the best product in the market, but if you don't know how to promote it or make business sense with it, then you're nowhere. Then I pitched to the trust for funding and they gave me a £4,000 loan. The pitch meeting was really good, it was like Dragons' Den. "You say you're going to make fifty grand this year. How are you going to do it?" It was much better than getting a

bank loan because I had to fully explain myself and I got a mentor. So, with the money I got a better van and got a whole set of gas equipment. I managed to turn it into the business it needed to be for the business plan to work.'

Carol, DEENEY'S

ACCOUNTS KEY POINTS

- Organisation is key.

- Knowledge is power.

- There are lots of finance options that can provide more than just money.

Chapter 10

What happens when things go wrong?

I hate to break it to you, but it won't all be smooth sailing, especially on your first day. Things will break, orders will be incorrect or undelivered, it'll rain for the whole of the summer or there'll be heavy snow in March. Staff will flake, your van will break down and you've just done your back in. Customers will be rude, market managers will be stressed out and yell at you and everything you own will, at one point, be coated in mud. Most of these things will happen to you and it's important to realise that:

1.   It's not only happening to you.

2.   Tomorrow will be a better day.

All of these things have happened to me and some of them all on the same day. Those days are awful, but you need to pick yourself up, get yourself home, get clean, have some food and a beer or a cup of tea and go to bed. Start the next day afresh. If you let each bad event weigh you down you will go mad and end up a shell of a human.

Don't panic – you learn quickly on the job. All it takes is a few bad services where nothing is working or you forget half your stock, and you will find a way to make it better. If you're standing there not selling anything, you become pretty desperate to work out a way to make money and you *will*, you'll figure it out.

I have a notebook filled with to-do lists, and looking back through them it's amazing to see stuff that regularly appeared on my lists just a few months ago that doesn't even make it to my lists now, because I'm constantly learning and then I start doing it automatically. When you first start you will have many, many lists – remember this, email that person, set this up and cook that – and then suddenly those things become second nature to you. You don't need to remind yourself to do a bread order or go to the bank because you fall into a routine and do those things automatically. I would highly recommend lists, especially at the start. If you're feeling overwhelmed at any point and feel like you've got too much to do, then write it all down as a list and just start working your way through it all. You will find that some of it is really quick and easily solved, and the rest can be broken down into more manageable chunks. Embrace the list!

Make an action plan so that whatever bad happened before won't be as likely to happen again. Some things, like the weather, may seem like they're out of your hands completely, but you *can* plan for them. Keep an eye on the forecast and order stock accordingly. Make sure your van is weatherproof and that your gazebo is weighted down. Make sure that your service is slick and top-notch and then, if someone does complain, you know that they're just an angry prick and it's not on you. Double-check your orders, get your van fixed, don't rely on being lucky, stop using unreliable staff.

'What will make or break you is the lack of preparation. Simple stuff. Make sure your bread rolls are sliced (don't do them per customer) and make sure you've got enough gas. If you've got a trailer or a van, what is the tread on the tyres, what's your pressure on them, because if you get a flat on the way to an event, you're fucked. Accidents do happen, but bad maintenance on a van can mean you don't get to the show and so you don't make the money you need.'

Leo, NORTHFIELD FARM

All these things take time, money and energy, which you will lack in the early days of running a street-food stall. But if things start to fall apart around you and you can't work out why, take a moment. Make a list of everything that is going wrong and work out if you can find a solution for it. Taking the time to find solutions will save you hours, if not days, of stress down the line.

So, you get a bad review and you know you did everything right, but for some reason someone has decided to give you a shitty review anyway. That person doesn't realise that to you it feels like they are attacking everything you stand for, your very soul and all those hours of your life you have poured into the business. They're just pissed off and are looking for a fight. For this reason you shouldn't write a response straight away. Take some time before responding to anything negative. Once you have taken some time, write down a response and show it to a friend first. Don't make the situation worse by fuelling the fire. Complaints are best dealt with calmly. Once again, you're not in *Chef*.

Warning: If you are using a family recipe, make sure you can distance yourself from it emotionally if people say they don't like it or it takes too long, so you don't feel like they are personally insulting your granny and asking to be punched in the face. Punching your customers is not great for business. Or so I've heard.

And sometimes everything will just go wrong. An event will change the format, so you can't go back, or you get rejected from a market for no reason at all. People will often say, 'It's just business, don't take it personally'. This is complete bollocks. It is nigh-on impossible not to take it personally as the business is your baby. You can say, 'It's just business' when you're in a huge corporation and you've not got the deal you wanted, fine, no skin off your nose. But when it comes down to talking about your business, which you've built from the ground up, it's impossible not to take it personally. Don't feel stupid if you're completely gutted or you have a cry; your friends with the 'real' jobs will think that you're mad, but you're not. Often your friends can see your street-food business as a 'bit of fun' or a phase, so they don't get it when you're heartbroken after a shitty event. They don't see the money or the hours you've lost. Just bear in mind, every single street-food trader out there will have had a similar experience to yours. It's not just you, you're not useless; it can just be really hard sometimes.

'One event last year, one of us had had to come back to London for more stock. We took the refrigerated van key and then left it in London, so that when we got back to the festival we couldn't get into the fridge van. We've had so many fridge van issues, like staff who had been out all night unplugging the fridge van and then of course it drains the battery and you can't get into it. Staff going missing. We did a vegan event and I got to the unit and it had been broken into. It didn't look like anything had been taken, so I packed it all into the van (I had packed all the stock into cool boxes the night before), got to the event, set up and the cool boxes were completely empty – they'd nicked all the vegan cheese. Luckily it was in Shoreditch, so I managed to find some more! What I've learnt is that you never know what's going to go wrong and it can come at any moment. It's not very good for your blood pressure, but there's nothing really you can do about it. You do learn not to be fazed by things and not go into a meltdown. After a while you learn to say, "Okay, let's do this instead then." And things always all happen at once too.'

Anna and Tony, ANNA MAE'S

You learn a lot from failing. If I had been successful from the set-off, then I'd have nothing of use to tell you. Sometimes you have to fail at something a few times to really work out where you've gone wrong. As long as you learn a bit and don't die doing it, then it's fine, carry on. For street food to be a viable career for you, you need to relish the process rather than the rewards. You obviously need to make a living, but if your only aim is to be in magazines or be super-rich and you don't enjoy the process, then you'll be a broken person by the time you get there.

Don't get bogged down with the day-to-day running of the business. If you're constantly worried about your bread order, then your mind is not focused on the business itself and where it is going. Obviously, if you have a busy summer with twenty-three festivals then you won't have an option, but just make sure you take time before and afterwards to work out where you're going. It will also help put the day-to-day stresses into perspective and push you to take the next step.

'I wasn't prepared for how exhausting it would be. I always thought that opening my own business would give me more freedom and time, but actually you never switch off from it. I wish someone had prepared me mentally for how much you think about it. But you do learn to be better at that and not to care about some of the things you did care about at the beginning.'

Sophia, NONNA'S GELATO

Think about what you can bring most value to. In the end, the biggest source of capital in your business is your time, so spend it on activities that deliver the highest measurable return. Once you're in a position to employ staff, don't spend half the day doing their job for them. You need to be pushing the business forward, developing new products, meeting new market managers – whatever it is, make sure you're not being held back by your own business.

'It's a love-hate relationship. There are times when I'm working and I love it, and you're getting good feedback and that's why I do it, but then there are nights when I'm lying awake thinking, "I haven't paid that or him," or when you're knee-deep in chicken fat at a festival and you think, "What am I doing?" People think it's really cool and glamorous, but it's really not.'

Ronan, GINGER AND CHILLI

But in the end, it's all worth it . . .

'There's a lot more to it than you first think, but it does make you think, "This is our business, we've created it, so the hard work, the sweat and the tears, all the hours, it's all worth it," and it does make you so happy. Especially when you walk in, you're busy, your staff are happy and know what they're doing, the food's going out really well and you just think, "We've created this!" Especially here, it's very much about being part of the community, so that the B&B owners have another place

to recommend to their guests. It's a lovely feeling to know that we've brought another aspect to the village. And hopefully we're bringing more footfall to the village, benefitting the whole community.'

Fenella and Kirsty, THE SEAFOOD SHACK

WHEN THE GOING GETS TOUGH KEY POINTS

- Things will go wrong.

- Prepare better next time.

- Put the systems in place and your business will be a joy to run.

Chapter 11

Starting and finishing

It's massively brave to set up any business. To step sideways off the treadmill of life and often throw yourself backwards while all your friends are heading towards the next promotion, the next pay rise, the next job. To say 'Fuck it' to the security, career progression and monthly pay packet is quite mad. Even now, I find myself fascinated by other people's jobs: what they do all day, how many meetings they go to, whether the meetings are worth their time at all. How much people get paid, and for doing precisely what, often baffles and surprises me. Five years into our business I became pregnant, and in the early months, when everything felt slightly mad I went through a phase of googling different companies' maternity-leave policies just to seemingly prove to myself what a fool I'd been not to stay on the corporate ladder. I constantly googled 'Pregnant directors of small companies how long mat leave', as if such a concise question would provide me with a clear answer. It's pretty hard to work out if you're doing life 'right' in the best of circumstances, never mind when you're throwing away a monthly pay cheque all on a gamble that the sandwich you think it probably quite good will suddenly be able to pay all of your bills.

People have different priorities in life and different dreams. This is especially true in the street-food industry. For every business that wants to hit every festival in the country and have the winter off, there's one that's very happy doing the local markets and a bit of catering here and there, which fits in around their family. Work out what your priorities are before you set up and write them down somewhere. A year or so into the business, have a look again and see if you still agree. What are your priorities now? Are they different? If so, why? If you're not hitting your priorities, then work out how to do that and make a plan of action. Running a business is *bloody hard*, but it's even harder if you've neglected everything else you ever cared about. Sometimes you will have to make a hard choice between work and your personal life – don't we all? But if you find yourself having to make those difficult decisions more and more often, then it may not be worth it. People talk about 'success at all costs'. This is bollocks. Everyone knows that the rich guy in the fancy house with the big business is alone and miserable.

Running a business with your partner can be a joy but can also be an absolute nightmare, particularly at the start when you don't know what you're doing, you're stressed, tired and panicking about money. Then you discover that your partner is the worst colleague in the history of work colleagues. So you bicker and argue at work, hurling insults left and right, or just make snide asides throughout the day. And then you go home and realise unreasonable colleague lives there too. Absolute fucking nightmare. So don't expect it all to be sunshine and rainbows; you need to put the work in, set some boundaries and attempt to be reasonable with each other. We always said that from the start we'd always put the relationship first, which was complete smug bollocks. We didn't actually manage that until at least the second or third year. We woke up one day and realised that all we talked about was Shrimpy, and all we did was work and something had to give. It's a Catch-22 though because the same drive to make the business work is also the same drive that can make you neglect your relationship. Now we're much better at it; delegating and taking time off, but we're also just not as desperate to prove ourselves as we were six years ago. We're now more confident in ourselves and in our business.

It's a brave thing to set up a business, but it's a braver thing to stop. People think it shows them as weak, but really it takes huge guts to say, 'Look, I tried my hardest, but it didn't work'. Sometimes you may have had one too many bad events and find yourself £10,000 down. You may have lost a permanent spot, or the organisers have raised the rents to an obscene amount, or, maybe, no matter what you tried, people just didn't buy your food. It's fine. It's crap but it's fine. You gave it a go, which shows you're a hard worker, creative, willing to take risks, and that you think outside the box. Employers love that, it looks great on your CV. Also, the relief once it's all over is amazing. I have seen loads of businesses come and go and the former owners will sometimes come back to the markets they had been on to have a poke around. They look so much more relaxed now that they're not slogging their guts out every

Saturday morning. They're relaxed because they know that, no matter what, they have a wage coming in every month and it's not going to take every single hour of the day, sleepless nights and all the hustle they've got to get it. It's only now that they have that perspective. People have gone on to have really interesting jobs, start families or even moved countries all because their businesses closed. They are all loving it. Yes, of course, it's heartbreaking if something which you've poured two, three, seven years of your life into turns into nothing, but there are other roads. Don't flog a dead horse. There's life outside street food.

'Even in these troubled times, people ask if I regret not having a secure job and pay, but I completely don't. Yes, it's a heartache, and yes, instability, and yes, a lot of us in this industry could lose our dream, but we've made a difference, we've followed our heart and our passion.'

Ranie, JAH JYOT

Having said that, for approximately every hundred businesses there's one that hits the big time. Whether it's going from selling marshmallows at a market stall in east London to being stocked in every Sainsbury's in the country, or Honest Burger starting off with £5,000 in a gazebo and going on to open hundreds of stores nationwide. You could create a cult following like BAO, who started on a market stall and now have queues round the block for their restaurants; or a Pizza Pilgrims story, who went from a Piaggio at a £10 market stall to multiple restaurants. Success is possible, but you've got to work really bloody hard and have at least a small bit of luck thrown in to make it happen.

When I feel disheartened with the business, I listen to an amazing podcast called *How I Built This*. Guy Raz talks to people who set up companies which are now huge. It makes you realise that you're not alone, and that whatever mad thing you're doing to make the business work is fine, because someone else has done something equally mad. There are amazing stories in there about how people made it up as they went along, got rejected for loans and made everything in a garage with their gran. If you're having a dispiriting day they're great to listen to to give you a little boost. They all have some pretty horrific stories in them, but they show that every business has its struggles.

But, surely, it's worth giving it a go? You never know what might be at the end of the rainbow, and think of the adventures you'll have!

Sign-off: Shrimp up your life

I set up Shrimpy with my partner back in 2013. We were both desperate to be independent and wanted to see how far we could go on our own. After a trial on Camden Market we were offered a spot, so both quit our jobs and learned along the way. We made so many bad decisions in our first year and made so little money that it's quite unbelievable how we managed to carry on, rather than just crawl back to our old jobs. Drive might be a word for it, but stubbornness is probably a more accurate term. A distinct lack of a 'plan B' was also a big factor.

Looking back on the early days of the business it's completely mad what we did. We were young and foolish, and we became completely obsessed with this idea and did everything to make it work. Most of which was just ignoring how badly it was all going. We went from having good, steady, well-paid jobs to scraping by and just making rent. We both took on second jobs so we were working continuously. I remember the first Christmas: the thing I was most looking forward to was the five-hour car journey back home to Durham because it was the first time for three months that I'd had a chance to just sit and not do anything.

We used to take the bus to Billingsgate fish market as we didn't have a car, let alone a van. We'd get there at half-four in the morning, buy the fish and then carry it back on the bus on our knees. Some buses wouldn't let us on, shockingly, with polystyrene boxes of fish, so we had to wait and hope that the next one would. Once we got home we'd prep everything then jump on the 214 bus to Camden, carrying our boxes of shrimp in the hope we'd make £100. It was *complete* madness. Who runs a street-food business on a bus? Spring came around and we worked out it was cheaper to cycle to the market so we'd cycle to and from Camden with our shrimp, and whatever else we needed, in our baskets.

I'm amazed we survived. We managed it because of the community we found there – forty stallholders in the west yard, all completely deranged in their own special way. You were welcomed into the fold, everyone helped each other, we stood in the rain together, we helped each other out of scrapes, gave each other business and life advice, and had storage parties together.

We even set up other businesses at one point or another because we thought they would be easier. First there was 'Bloody Eddies', which sounds like an awful period product, but was actually chips with Bolognese and Bloody Mary sauce. It was delicious but not who we wanted to be as a brand. We could have been filmed in the first two years as floundering idiots. It's at times like these that it would have been helpful if we'd actually written a business plan to work out who we were and what we wanted to do, instead of changing it every day and becoming panicked about paying our rent. The second was called 'Grainiacs', which were healthy grain bowls we sold to office workers. It was a bit shit and we knew it. We shoved it together to try to make some easy money and then spent the whole time apologising for it, hating it and telling people to ignore it because Shrimpy was the real deal. I'm not sure if you know anything about how to run a business but that isn't it.

Yes, Shrimpy is a pain sometimes, and sometimes we see other businesses who seemingly have an easier life, and why on earth did we *ever* think that selling seafood on the street was going to be easy (especially seven years ago)? But we are proud of our product and we've finally worked out how to do it.

I think that success is connected with being perpetually dissatisfied with your business. If you think it's all perfect, then you're mad. No one's business model is 100 per cent perfect, especially in street food. There's always something that works better than something else, or that only works in certain places. That's fine; it wouldn't do for us all to be the same. It's good if you're dissatisfied with your business. Use that dissatisfaction to make it better, rather than turning it into a whole new venture.

We now have decent weekend spots on Southbank Centre Food Market and Broadway Market and a seven-day kiosk in a food hall in Old Spitalfields Market. We've done many other markets along the way, all kinds of mad events and a few festivals thrown in there too.

Who knows where we'll be after Covid-19, but part of the beauty of street food is that you can just start all over again. We are all used to shutting up shop for extended periods of time (winter) and finding opportunities, where before there were none. Street-food businesses didn't qualify for the majority of the government help, which has made things difficult, but because of the flexible nature of street food a lot of us will be in a much better position than restaurants to start again. Once lockdown ended we were able to just go and set up the gazebo and start again. So give it a go; it's comparatively cheap, flexible and very, very exciting. It's delicious freedom.

Acknowledgements

Thank you to all the businesses I interviewed. You could have been doing literally anything else, but you gave me your time and you were so wise.

Thank you to my family, whose support and enthusiasm for my schemes seems unending.